SOUTH WALES
RAILWAYS GALLERY

Front cover: Without doubt, South Wales, steam, rail and coal is captured in this classic scene. Staged in 1930 for publicity purposes, 6662 and 6676 each haul a trainload of Best Welsh Steam Coal while far left a third train with returning empties is likely headed by another 56XX, reflecting a typical everyday scene at Taff's Well. The Barry Railway's Walnut Tree Viaduct shares the panorama. *(Great Western Trust)*

Back cover top: The 42XXs were built specifically for the short runs of heavy Coal trains in South Wales. The Stock Market Crash of 1929 saw coal traffic dramatically fall so the decision was taken to rebuild 54 of them with extended coal carrying capacity for greater range and usefulness. This added 4 feet to the frames, requiring the addition of a trailing wheel set, making them 2-8-2Ts. Weighing in at 92¾ tons, 7222 features here in Aberdare shed yard. With 6 tons of coal in the bunker, a round trip from Aberdare to Salisbury would be well within her range. 26 August 1964. *(D.K. Jones-Cresselley Collection)*

Back cover bottom: The end of an era. This was the very last regular steam worked passenger train from South Wales recorded at Bridgend on Saturday, 5 September 1964. 6838 *Goodmoor Grange*, with ten coaches, departs at 11.07am (16 minutes late) on the 9.10 SO Llanelly to Bournemouth and Brockenhurst. 6838 worked as far as Westbury; there a BR Standard Class 5 took over, ran as far as Dorchester Junction and was relieved by another Standard Class 5. *(courtesy Brian Lewis)*

SOUTH WALES
RAILWAYS GALLERY

STUART DAVIES

PEN & SWORD
TRANSPORT

AN IMPRINT OF PEN & SWORD BOOKS LTD.
YORKSHIRE - PHILADELPHIA

First published in Great Britain in 2022 by
Pen and Sword Transport
An imprint of
Pen & Sword Books Ltd.
Yorkshire – Philadelphia

ISBN 978 1 52677 601 3

Typeset in 11/13 Palatino by SJmagic DESIGN SERVICES, India.

Printed and bound by Printworks Global Ltd, London/Hong Kong.

Pen & Sword Books Ltd incorporates the imprints of Pen & Sword Books Archaeology, Atlas, Aviation, Battleground, Discovery, Family History, History, Maritime, Military, Naval, Politics, Railways, Select, Transport, True Crime, Fiction, Frontline Books, Leo Cooper, Praetorian Press, Seaforth Publishing, Wharncliffe and White Owl.

For a complete list of Pen & Sword titles please contact

PEN & SWORD BOOKS LIMITED
47 Church Street, Barnsley, South Yorkshire, S70 2AS, England
E-mail: enquiries@pen-and-sword.co.uk
Website: www.pen-and-sword.co.uk

or

PEN AND SWORD BOOKS
1950 Lawrence Rd, Havertown, PA 19083, USA
E-mail: Uspen-and-sword@casematepublishers.com
Website: www.penandswordbooks.com

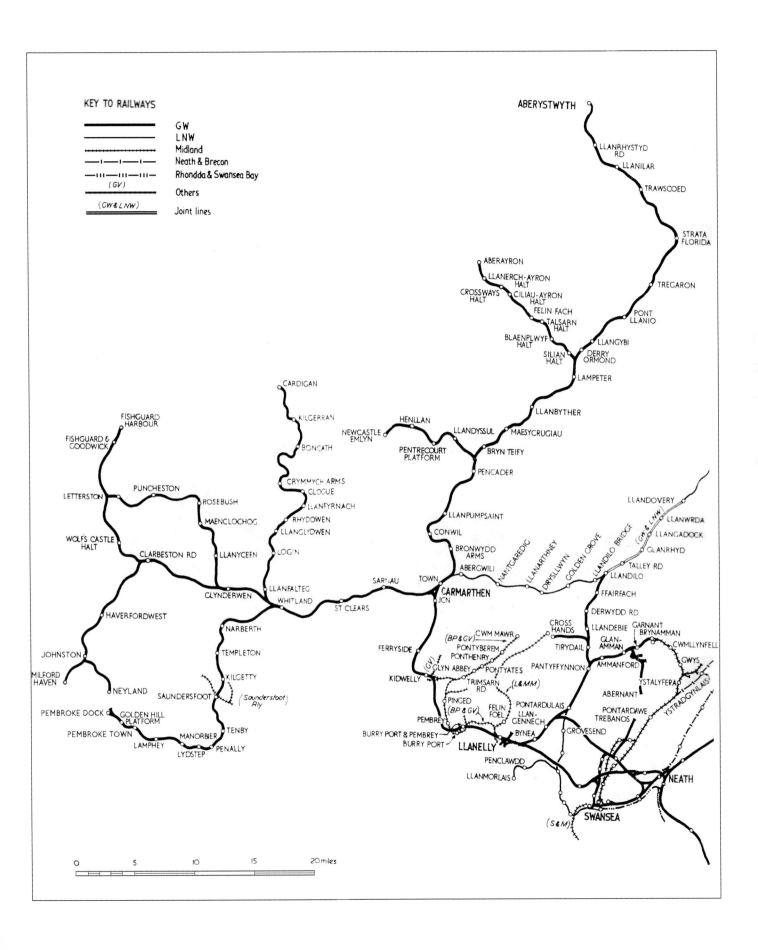

KEY TO RAILWAYS

GW
LNW
Midland
Neath & Brecon
Rhondda & Swansea Bay
(GV) Others
(GW&LNW) Joint lines

ABERYSTWYTH

LLANRHYSTYD RD
LLANILAR
TRAWSCOED
STRATA FLORIDA
TREGARON
PONT LLANIO
ABERAYRON
LLANERCH-AYRON HALT
CROSSWAYS HALT
CILIAU-AYRON HALT
FELIN FACH
TALSARN HALT
BLAENPLWYF HALT
SILIAN HALT
LLANGYBI
DERRY ORMOND
LAMPETER
LLANBYTHER
CARDIGAN
KILGERRAN
HENLLAN
LLANDYSSUL
MAESYCRUGIAU
NEWCASTLE EMLYN
BONCATH
PENTRECOURT PLATFORM
BRYN TEIFY
PENCADER
LLANDOVERY
FISHGUARD HARBOUR
CRYMMYCH ARMS
CLOGUE
LLANFYRNACH
LLANPUMPSAINT
LLANWRDA
LLANGADOCK
GLANRHYD
FISHGUARD & GOODWICK
PUNCHESTON
ROSEBUSH
RHYDOWEN
CONWIL
BRONWYDD ARMS
TALLEY RD
LETTERSTON
MAENCLOCHOG
LLANGLYDWEN
LLANDILO BRIDGE
LLANDILO
WOLFS CASTLE HALT
CLARBESTON RD
LLANYCEFN
LOGIN
ABERGWILI
FFAIRFACH
NANTGAREDIG
LLANARTHNEY
DRYSLLWYN
GOLDEN GROVE
LLANFALTEG
SARNAU
TOWN
CARMARTHEN
DERWYDD RD
CLYNDERWEN
WHITLAND
JCN
HAVERFORDWEST
ST CLEARS
CROSS HANDS
LLANDEBIE
GARNANT
BRYNAMMAN
CWMLLYNFELL
NARBERTH
CWM MAWR
TIRYDAIL
GLAN-AMMAN
GWYS
JOHNSTON
TEMPLETON
FERRYSIDE
(BP&GV)
PONTYBEREM
PONTHENRY
PANTYFFYNNON
AMMANFORD
MILFORD HAVEN
KILGETTY
(GV)
GLYN ABBEY
PONTYATES
YSTALYFERA
NEYLAND
SAUNDERSFOOT
(Saundersfoot Rly)
KIDWELLY
TRIMSARN RD
(L&MM)
ABERNANT
PEMBROKE DOCK
GOLDEN HILL PLATFORM
TENBY
PINGED
(BP&GV)
FELIN FOEL
PONTARDULAIS
PONTARDAWE
TREBANOS
YSTRADGYNLAIS
PEMBROKE TOWN
MANORBIER
PEMBREY
LLAN-GENNECH
GROVESEND
LAMPHEY
LYDSTEP
PENALLY
BURRY PORT & PEMBREY
BURRY PORT
BYNEA
LLANELLY
PENCLAWDD
(S&M)
LLANMORLAIS
NEATH
SWANSEA

0   5   10   15   20 miles

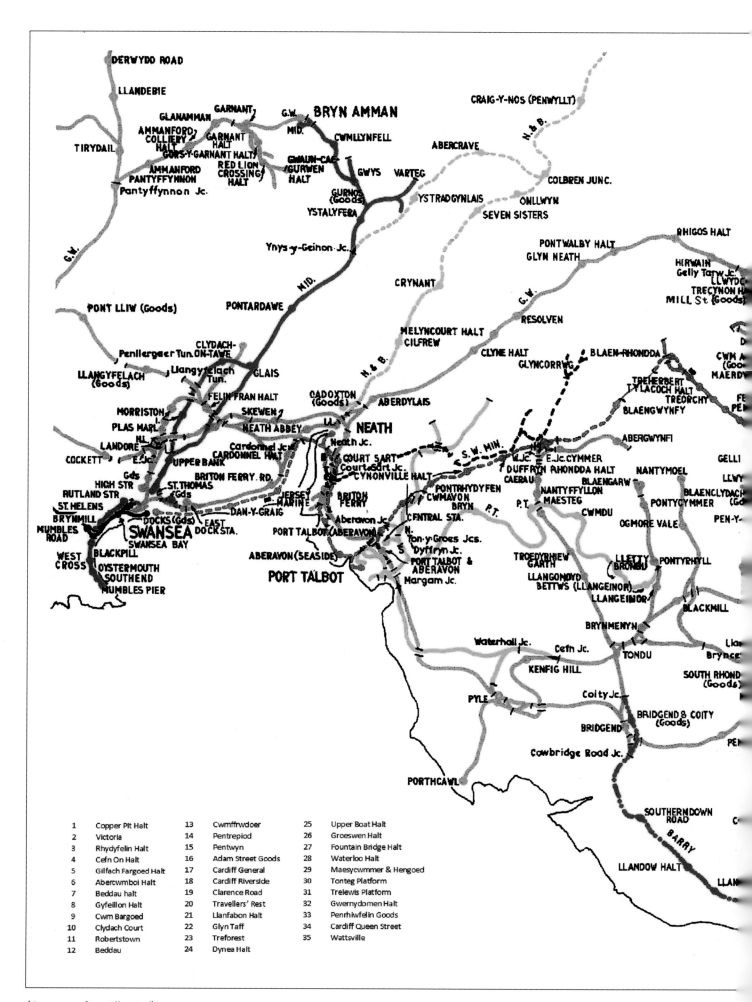

1	Copper Pit Halt	13	Cwmffrwdoer	25	Upper Boat Halt
2	Victoria	14	Pentrepiod	26	Groeswen Halt
3	Rhydyfelin Halt	15	Pentwyn	27	Fountain Bridge Halt
4	Cefn On Halt	16	Adam Street Goods	28	Waterloo Halt
5	Gilfach Fargoed Halt	17	Cardiff General	29	Maesycwmmer & Hengoed
6	Abercwmboi Halt	18	Cardiff Riverside	30	Tonteg Platform
7	Beddau halt	19	Clarence Road	31	Trelewis Platform
8	Gyfeillon Halt	20	Travellers' Rest	32	Gwernydomen Halt
9	Cwm Bargoed	21	Llanfabon Halt	33	Penrhiwfelin Goods
10	Clydach Court	22	Glyn Taff	34	Cardiff Queen Street
11	Robertstown	23	Treforest	35	Wattsville
12	Beddau	24	Dynea Halt		

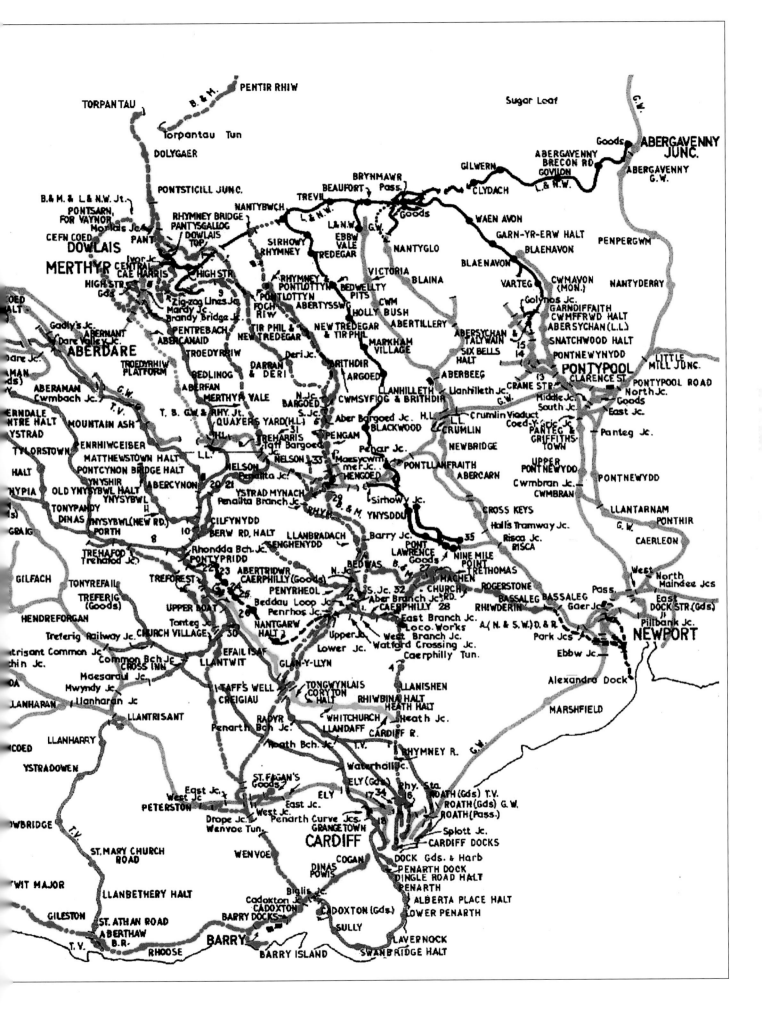

INTRODUCTION

The railway network South Wales once hosted (principally for the transportation of its coal from Pithead to blast furnace or port) was arguably one of the most complex in the world. Whilst some rationalisation of duplicate routes and closures were undertaken after 1923, the greater part of the network was extant until the early 1960s even though its prime revenue generator had long since peaked at 57 million tons in 1913. Indeed, it was always the bane of the coal authorities that rail moved more coal than they raised due to the additional movements from pithead to washeries.

To the unknowing, the inevitable concept is one of coal trains and yes, there was an abundance. There was little glamour or worthwhile publicity material with no Riviera to promote but the coffers of the railways overflowed with 'Arian' from the movement of the freight. Whereas other areas of the British network may claim similarities, what made South Wales unique until the mid-1980s was that its revenues far exceeded theirs.

Take away that thick coating and underneath lies a rich seam of unsung, unknown and unrecognised features that can claim many firsts in railway annals. On 21 February 1804 for example, Richard Trevithick's *Locomotive* ran from the Penydarren works, Merthyr, to Navigation House near Abercynon. This momentous journey made for a 100-guinea wager between two prominent Merthyr Ironmasters, Samuel Homfray and Richard Crawshay, but was never honoured.

Divisional Movements Inspector Tom Holloway best summed it all up. When introduced to a newly promoted supervisor, the newcomer was told he could 'forget the adage, all shipshape and Bristol fashion because there was nothing over there that we haven't got over here, except we've got a lot more of it'. Yet, in addition to all this coal, it is now even more difficult to appreciate that prior to the mid-1950s, every conceivable commodity was transported by rail. There was the Palethorpe's sausage van from Kidderminster to Cardiff, the Bowyer's Wiltshire pork sausage van from Trowbridge to Porthcawl, McVitie's Biscuits, Lyons Cakes, the overnight newspapers from London. The counties of Cardigan, Carmarthen and Pembroke supplied Londoners with almost 2 million pints of milk, whilst Milford Haven consigned 200 tons of fish each day. Oh! and did someone mention elephants?

The Great Western presence was almost entirely East to West whereas the many Welsh railway companies that were established ran North to South, the topography enhancing locomotive capabilities in favour of the loaded traffic down grade and empties up. As the valley floors were already spoken for, the Barry Railway, as a relative latecomer, constructed its railway at higher contour levels. This it achieved with no little grandeur, spanning the valleys with imposing viaducts, evading steep gradients and providing four tracking at stations so the heavy mineral trains ran unimpeded by stopping passenger services. Illustrating this grandeur, the Barry Railway:

- Was the only South Wales Railway to operate steamer services
- Imported five locomotives in kit form from Cooke Locomotive works of New Jersey and these were assembled Dockside and put into traffic 6 days after arrival at Barry

- Did not serve a single colliery direct
- Operated a Port to Port express through to Newcastle
- Was the first railway in Britain to operate 0-8-2T engines.

Great Western lines were designated Up to Paddington, Down to Swansea in accord with convention but the Welsh Companies matched the topography; it was Up to the heads of the valleys (this remained under the GW) so, the complexity presented a challenge when determining which was the Up Line and which was Down.

Each railway company purchased their locomotives from private builders. Some have been critical of the state of these 829 machines at the Grouping in 1923 and it is true to reflect that Swindon scrapped swathes of non-standard machines soon afterwards. However, many classes survived to pass into British Railways ownership and the successful Great Western 56XX Class that was introduced in 1926 without extensive trials with a prototype, was based on the Rhymney's 'R' Class. The former Rhymney locomotive works at Caerphilly was extensively enhanced by the GW to become the Welsh 'Swindon' and despite a zealous standardisation policy, persisted in turning out overhauled locomotives with brass safety valve bonnets when Swindon decreed they should be painted green.

To capitalise on the lucrative coal traffic, both the LNW and Midland Railways frequently courted several of the South Wales Companies establishing traffic agreements, joint lines and working arrangements but only ever succeeded in collecting crumbs off the table. As an illustration of how lucrative the traffic was, Swansea Docks supported two main lines running parallel to each other from Jersey Marine right through the docks and out the other side but to add to the complexity, these swapped sides by means of a grade separated junction at Danygraig.

In addition to the Cambrian, Great Western (GW), London & North Western (LNW) and Midland Railway (MR), fifteen independent companies were established in South Wales. At the 1923 Grouping, six of these became constituents of the enhanced GW:

A(N&SW) D&R**	Alexandra (Newport & South Wales) Docks & Railway
BR**	Barry Railway
Cam	Cambrian Railways
Cardiff**	Cardiff Railway
RR	Rhymney Railway
TVR**	Taff Vale Railway

The remainder became subsidiaries of the GW:

B&M	Brecon & Merthyr Railway
BP&GV	Burry Port & Gwendraeth Valley Railway
GVR	Gwendraeth Valley Railway
Ll &MM	Llanelly & Mynydd Mawr Railway
N&B	Neath & Brecon Railway
PTR**	Port Talbot Railway
R&SB**	Rhondda & Swansea Bay Railway
SWMR	South Wales Mineral Railway
SHT	Swansea Harbour Trust
P&M	Powlesland & Mason

** denotes Railway Company with Dock ownership

The abbreviations above are used throughout the book together with:

SWML	South Wales Main Line (Chepstow to Neyland)
VoN	Vale of Neath (Pontypool Road to Neath General) (GW)
VoG	Vale of Glamorgan (Barry Railway)
MT&A	Merthyr Tredegar & Abergavenny (LNW)
SB	Signal Box
GF	Ground frame
Jcn	Junction
HL/LL	High Level/Low Level

To add to the complexity of the network just look at a short selection of stations and depots established to serve the communities:

Dowlais Top, Dowlais Cae Harris, Dowlais Furnace Top, Dowlais High Street & Dowlais Central
Cwmavon (Monmouthshire), Cwmavon (Glamorgan)
Pentrefelin (Mon), Pentrefelin (Glam)
Pengam (Mon), Pengam (Glam), Pengam (Cardiff)
Monmouth Troy, Monmouth May Hill
Clydach (MT&A), Clydach (MR)

Then add some poetic idylls:

Quakers' Yard, Nelson, Upper Boat, Birchgrove, Dingle Road, Blackwood, Oakdale, Ferndale, Walnut Tree, Taff's Well, Blackmill, Brandy Bridge, Copper Pit, Swanbridge, Alberta Place, Mountain Ash, Cardiff Road and Oxford Street, Pyle, White Hart, Fountain Bridge, Waterloo, Sebastopol, Darren & Deri, Beaufort, Bassaleg, Nine Mile Point, Fleur de Lys, Bournville, Maliphant, Cockett, Strata Florida, Golden Grove, Courtybella, Mendalgief (East & West).

and of course, some False Teeth Falsettos:

Fochrhiw, Pentir Rhiw, Troedyrhiw, Talybont, Talyllyn, Torpantau, Gilfach Goch, Gilfach Fargoed, Hendreforgan, Nantyffyllon, Pantysgallog, Pontlottyn, Pontsticill, Pochin, Pontllanfraith (HL & LL connected by Bird in Hand East and West Junctions), Gwernydomen, Groesffordd, Trerhyngyll and Llettybrongu (its literal translation 'hill crest dwelling').

As to the main traffic, in 1864 a government committee, at the insistence of MPs from constituencies in the NE of England coalfield, recommended that in future, Naval contracts should specify a mixture of ⅔ Welsh, ⅓ Newcastle Coals. After complaints from the Navy, the Admiralty reverted to the exclusive use of Aberdare Dry Steam Coal from 1872.

In 1913, 57 million tons of coal were raised by hand in South Wales. 37 million tons were exported via the Docks of which 11 million tons went through Barry (the greatest quantity of any port in Britain).

In 1920, the South Wales Coalfield employed 271,000 men and at the formation of the NCB in 1947, there were 135 collieries employing 33,750 men.

Another challenge today is to appreciate just how extensive the network was. Municipal planners have done their best to obliterate many of the former trackbeds. Many know the A465 trunk-road as 'The Heads of the Valleys', though few now realise most of it was once a main line railway. The Chief Roster Clerk at Margam was somewhat amused when he realised his new house had been built on Duffryn Yard's Turntable.

To make matters worse, time removes the advantage of living memories. Fortunately, a number of repositories have in their depths thousands of illustrations recording the South Wales network but even so many photographs are sadly without identity. Nonetheless, the volunteers in these sources are more than happy to supply any amount of material and as a result, a few hitherto unpublished nuggets have emerged.

I am grateful particularly to the following for their help, support and encouragement: John Hodge, Keith Jones (Cresselley Collection), Brian Lewis, Gerald Nichols (Stephenson Locomotive Society), Mike Roach, Peter Waller (Online Transport Archive) and Laurence Waters (Great Western Trust).

Every effort has been made to accredit all the illustrations to the photographers concerned. Where this has not been possible, they should contact Stuart Davies to repair the situation. (davies469@aol.com)

This Gallery attempts to give a wider appreciation of what South Wales Railways had to offer. The images of Coal Trains are thus deliberately restrained as are specific portraits of locomotive classes. Both of these would fill a volume by themselves. Further, to deliver any geographical order when East-West arteries were criss-crossed by a grid of North-South routes that in themselves were Main Lines, some even quadrupled, is also difficult. Instead, a number of themes have been adopted and a scattergun approach applied to deliver this. Similarly, the LNW and MR, then in 1923 LMS, are represented but as in reality, their pictorial presence is proportionate. It is hoped you enjoy the outcome and if so, all the effort has been worthwhile.

Aerial view of the railway gateways to South Wales from 1886. The Severn Tunnel left (4 miles 624 Yards) and the original 1850 route of the South Wales main line via Gloucester right. In the top distance can be seen the junction for the Sudbrook branch off to the right. Gradients within the tunnel are 1 in 90 Welsh side and 1 in 100 English side. The tunnel is 65ft below the riverbed, the river depth above is 55ft. Construction consisted of 76.5 million bricks, 37,000 tons of cement and cost £2m. Until recently, it was the longest underwater tunnel in the world. *(Author's collection)*

A French invasion. In 1903, Churchward (the GW's Chief Mechanical Engineer) obtained a De Glehn 4-cylinder compound from the Nord Railway of France for comparative trials. In 1905, two more were purchased and here we see 104, named *Alliance* in 1907, leaving the Severn Tunnel and making a rare sortie into Wales around 1912. *(A.C. Roberts)*

Under the tracks at the bottom of Severn Tunnel flows a small river, the source of which is unknown. To prevent flooding, a pumping station was established at Sudbrook, seen here with 6439 and a Stephenson Locomotive Society visit on 4 January 1959. Today the water is used in the Budweiser Brewery at Magor. *(Author's collection)*

Originally the pumping station employed six beam engines, one of which is seen here in 1959. They were replaced in the 1960s by electric pumps and remove 5 million gallons of water per day. *(Author's collection)*

A ventilation shaft with fan was fitted to extract fumes. It had a lift which enabled Severn Tunnel traincrews to effect shift changes when engineering trains occupied the tunnel for maintenance work. *(Author's collection)*

Car-carrying trains were operated between Severn Tunnel Junction and Pilning High Level until the opening of the Severn Road Suspension Bridge. 4130 has just left the tunnel with a car transporter train in 1962. Cars were conveyed for 22s 6d (return 35s), passengers 1s 9d (return 3s) and a tarpaulin to protect the vehicle from smut was an extra 2s. *(D.K. Jones/Cresselley collection)*

Severn Tunnel Junction was host to a Marshalling Yard with a history dating back to 1886. In its final form, it consisted of the Up or Bristol yard (shown here) and Downside Yard. In principle, the former dealt with Welsh to English traffic, the other vice versa. The two yards were separated by the Main Line which was a major operating headache with transfers of wagons between them necessitating a slot between trains on the main line. Yard Supervisor Jack Price always proudly wore his uniform peaked cap but in July 1978 was reduced to tears when forced to cancel a freight train through lack of sidelamps. *(Great Western Trust)*

Trains were propelled over a hump where a shunter would uncouple the individual portions according to destination and the detachment would then gravitate into the designated siding. Another shunter (referred to as a runner) would run alongside the raft of loose wagons and if their speed became excessive, insert a 'Brakestick' between solebar and brake handle of the wagon(s) thus applying the handbrake(s). There were two runners provided on each of the Up and, illustrated here, Down humps. The wagon is a Coil E fitted with nylon hoods to protect the high value Cold Reduced Steel Coil (used in the making of cars and white electrical goods) from getting wet. These wagons were clearly stencilled 'Not to be Hump or Loose Shunted,' so it is to be hoped this one was empty. The automated points in the yard worked by compressed air and when operated, hissed at you. *(Author's collection)*

Water troughs existed at Magor and Ferryside enabling locomotives to pick up water with scoops. At Magor, a Hall on a Plymouth service replenishes her supply in April 1962. Too much water escaped through the tender's overflow and if the leading vehicle's facing corridor connection was not blanked off with plates, passengers in the first compartments would get a soaking. *(Alan A. Jarvis 1337/Stephenson Locomotive Society)*

The Richard Thomas & Baldwins Steelworks at Llanwern opened in 1962. The hot strip mill pioneered the first successful use of a computer for complete mill control. At St Mellons, a 42XX heads a train of Steel Ingots from Margam for Llanwern works on 25 May 1963. Because Newport Docks had insufficient draught, iron ore was latterly conveyed by five 3,000-ton trains daily (the heaviest haul in Britain) from Port Talbot Docks but was the Achilles' heel of production at Llanwern. To stand lineside with the thundering passage of these Class 37 triple-headed mammoths was an unforgettable experience. *(Alan A. Jarvis 2269/Stephenson Locomotive Society)*

Newport station was rebuilt in 1929 along with new offices for the District Headquarters. Until the creation of the Cardiff Valleys following grouping in 1923, the only other District in South Wales was Neath. The Newport District was the largest in the UK both in terms of revenue and locomotive allocation. Motive Power Depots identified its geographical spread, Severn Tunnel Junction, Ebbw Junction (Newport), Pill (Newport Docks), Pontypool Road, Aberbeeg, Aberdare, Canton (Cardiff), Llantrisant and Tondu. Under BR, it was the most highly graded Motive Power Superintendent post. Ebbw Junction's BR Shedcode was 86A, a bone of contention at Canton (86C) who handled the more prestigious passenger work. *(Author's collection)*

The intensity of train movements at Newport was recognized by the installation of power signalling seen here at Newport East in 1929. When the next generation of Entrance/Exit Power Signal Boxes were introduced in the 1960s, the Western Region referred to them as Panel Signal Boxes whereas the other regions called them Power Signal Boxes. *(Author's collection)*

Newport Hillfield Tunnel to the west of the station was doubled in 1912 and the route from Severn Tunnel Junction to Cardiff West became a four-track layout throughout. *(Author's collection)*

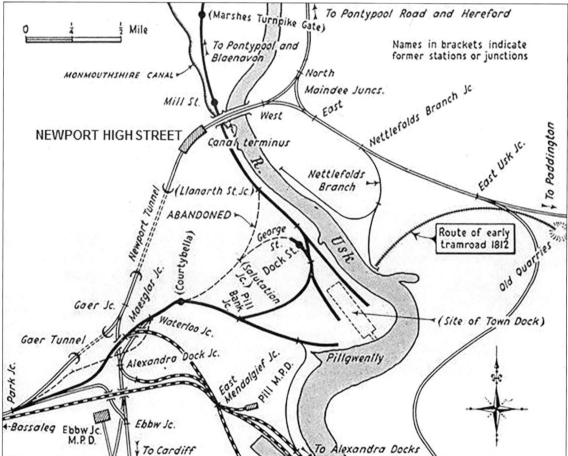

A map of the area showing the railway network in the immediate environs of Newport.

Above left: A train indicator board gives some idea of the range of destinations served from Newport. *(Author's collection)*

Above right: Newport was the focal point for several local services. Here at the end of the Eastern Valley at Blaenavon Low Level before returning to Newport, is 6429 and Auto train, 28 August 1957. *(R.W.A. Jones/Online Transport Archive)*

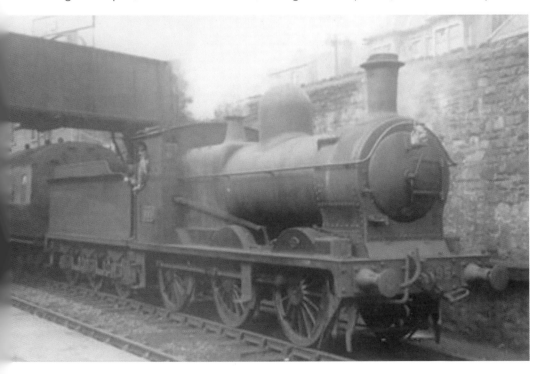

At first glance, a 3201 Dean Goods Class 0-6-0. However, our cop is an even rarer Cambrian 15 Class 0-6-0 No. 895 (Cambrian Railways 101) at Newport High St in 1949 with the 7.35am from Brecon. 895 will return to Brecon after servicing and turning at Ebbw Junction Shed at 11.15am. This was the furthest south these engines came, working a three-day cycle Oswestry Brecon, Brecon Newport Brecon and finally Brecon Oswestry. Originally fifteen in number, three were scrapped in 1923 at Grouping, one was lost at Friog in 1933 when a rockfall caused its derailment and fall to the shore way below. The remaining eleven passed into BR ownership, the last withdrawn in October 1954. *(Author's collection)*

On a regular basis, 'foreign' engines appeared at Newport and Tredegar shed was the source of most with LNW Sirhowy Valley services. In 1955, the former LMS (LNW & MR) lines in South Wales were transferred to the Western Region, who soon set about replacing the indigenous machines. In this 18 June 1959 view of the shed, 6600 & 7721 are on hand with native tenants 41204 and 41201. *(R.W.A. Jones/Online Transport Archive)*

The oldest deep mine colliery in the South Wales Coalfield was at Aberaman near Aberdare which opened in 1837. *(Author's collection)*

In many cases, an internal railway network linked pithead to railhead. The largest was the former North's Navigation system at Maesteg and the upper reaches of the Llynfi Valley originally constructed to serve the Iron Works there. It extended to Caerau running parallel to the GW line albeit at a higher level. In later years this was further extended when the former Port Talbot Railway from Maesteg to Cwmdu transferred to NCB operation. The scene here is the weighbridge of St John's Colliery at Cwmdu and 0-6-0T *Pamela*, Hunslet works No.3840 of 1956. *(Author's collection)*

A once traditional South Wales scene. With colliery in the background, auto fitted 6412 and former Cardiff Railway trailers W142 & W144 at Senghenydd, 21 May 1952. In the greatest mining disaster of all time, 439 men and boys lost their lives there in 1913. *(R.W.A. Jones/Online Transport Archive)*

Tirpentwys Colliery Pontypool. The deep and narrow mining valleys of Glamorgan and Monmouthshire severely constricted the layout of colliery sidings. This was one reason why they were located in or near the Docks at Cardiff 'Barry' Newport and Swansea where coal traffic could be staged. Blending of the various grades of coal was undertaken at these locations which involved intensive shunting before the traffic was called forward for shipping. *(Author's collection)*

By contrast, the anthracite coalfield lay under the gentle rolling vales of eastern Carmarthenshire, where more extensive siding facilities were possible. Ammanford Colliery 1912. *(Author's collection)*

In South Wales, privately owned wagons in a wonderful array of liveries were employed by most of the collieries or coal factors. When empty each had to be sorted before returning to their respective part of the coalfield. Maesglas Sidings, Newport viewed from Maesglas Jcn SB 1920s. *(Great Western Trust)*

Coal hoists in the Docks were only capable of tipping one wagon at a time so the wagons in each train had to be uncoupled beforehand. Similarly, wagons then had to be recoupled when released empty from the tipplers. To ship the tonnage offered daily throughout the year somewhere in Cardiff docks (seen here), a wagon was tipped every 30 seconds. *(Author's collection)*

Cadoxton (for Barry Docks). The Home Signal at Cadoxton North Signal Box (giving entry into the yard) was fitted with a unique indicator board. Operated by the signalman, this identified the siding in which the incoming train was to be deposited and the siding where the locomotive was to collect its returning train of empties having run round by means of the engine release road. As a whole, some 50m tons of coal was being raised annually. The highest was 1913, with 57m tons of which 37m tons were exported via the docks. Barry docks shipped 11m tons of this amount, the greatest quantity of any port in Britain. Emigration from England to Wales at the turn of the nineteenth century was second only to that to the US. *(Great Western Trust)*

Swansea Docks Burrows No.4 Set Sidings. *(Great Western Trust)*

Although staged for publicity purposes, this 1930 portrait reflects a typical everyday scene at Taff's Well where 6662 and 6676 each haul a trainload of Best Welsh Steam Coal and 'far left' a third train with returning empties likely headed by another 56XX. The Barry Railway's Walnut Tree Viaduct shares the panorama. *(Great Western Trust)*

Above left: The traditional means of coal tipping demonstrated here at Newport Docks. The wagon is a 10-ton wooden bodied type with end doors but at one end only. The railways had to ensure the wagon doors were the right way round to facilitate tipping at the coal hoist, individual wagons were presented in the right order to enable blending and the empty wagons were returned to the owning colliery. Shunting was therefore a continual process with large numbers of locomotives maintained purely to trip between the nearby holding sidings and the dockside coal hoists. *(Author's collection)*

Above right: Sir Felix Pole, General Manager, GWR, introduced large numbers of 20-ton, steel bodied wagons in 1924 to maximise productivity much to the disquiet of the coal factors. The view here shows the tipping of these wagons, in this case at Port Talbot Docks. *(Author's collection)*

Below: Another innovation introduced at this time at Port Talbot Docks was the loading of coal by electric conveyor belt. *(Author's collection)*

On 18 April 1946, Taff Vale A Class 365, hauling an early morning workmen's train, became derailed on Croeserw Viaduct on the R&SBR between Blaengwynfi and Cymmer and descended into the narrow ravine below, seen here soon afterwards. Due to the confined space, the locomotive was dismantled to enable its recovery. Fortunately, there were no fatalities and being a Treherbert favourite, 365 was back in traffic a few months later. (*Great Western Trust*)

Avon Colliery, Abergwynfi is seen here on Saturday, 21 November 1964, the occasion of a society special from Swansea worked by 9678 before continuing to Glyncorrwg, Blaengarw and Nantymoel, finally returning to Swansea High St. The colliery was unique in that it was owned by the GWR until 1947 when it was absorbed into the newly established NCB. (*Author's collection*)

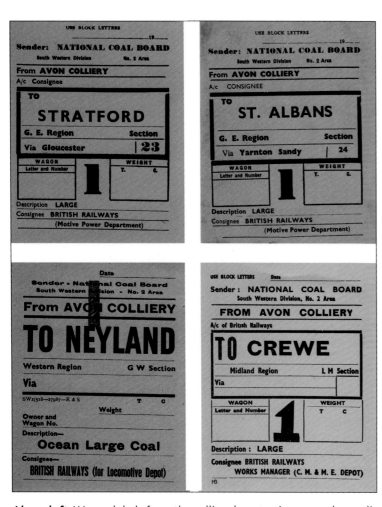

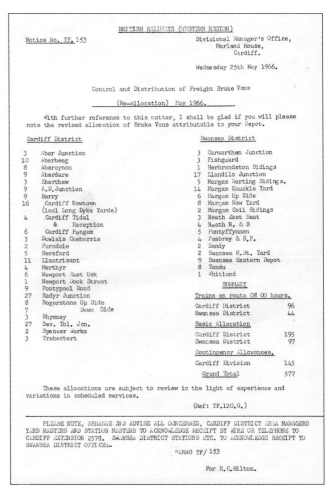

Above left: Wagon labels from the colliery bear testimony to the quality of coal for steam engines.

Above right: This 1966 disposition of Freight Brakevans in South Wales reflects the volume of traffic still handled at this time.

The Coal Exchange Building, Mount Stuart Square, Cardiff. The location where the coal factors sold their wares, the first £1m contract was awarded and the first £1m cheque was signed. By Royal Assent, in 1956 Cardiff was declared capital of Wales yet in 1825, the population of Merthyr Tydfil was ten times greater. *(Author's collection)*

A fascinating study of King's Dock Swansea at the turn of the twentieth century with seven coal hoists in view. Swansea had long been established as a metal working area and its port is much older than Cardiff. Much of its coal export was anthracite from the Western edge of the coalfield. *(Great Western Trust)*

The A(N&SW)D&RC purchased three second-hand bogie coaches from E.E. Cornforth in 1909. These were American style with end verandas and previously formed part of the Barnum & Bailey Circus Train. Two passed into GW ownership and were not withdrawn until 1926. *(National Museum of Wales)*

BRECON & MERTHYR	
B. & M. & L. & N.W. JOINT	
GREAT WESTERN	
G.W. & TAFF VALE JOINT	
QUAKER'S YARD & MERTHYR JOINT	
(GREAT WESTERN & RHYMNEY)	
TAFF VALE	
PRIVATE LINES	

Railway Clearing House Map of Merthyr which was served by six Railways: B&M, Taff, RR, GW, LNW and Cambrian.

The B&M for the last half mile from Rhydycar Junction ran on VoN metals to reach Merthyr High Street. At Mardy Junction, seen here looking south on 13 April 1963, the Taff Vale comes in on the left. 9638, with banking assistance from 8723, passes over the VoN viaduct. *(Great Western Trust)*

Of the pre-grouping locos passing to the GW, 50 per cent (400/793) were 0-6-2Ts to which the GW added a further 186 with the Class 56XX. It was these, perhaps more than any other, that epitomised the typical South Wales engine. Only Llantrisant appears never to have had an allocation, neither did they feature prominently in the dock sheds of Cardiff or Swansea, nor in large numbers at those sheds and valleys monopolised by the GW before 1922 and then only at Aberdare after 1945. These handsome valley hybrids, embracing several features of the Rhymney R Class and Swindon practice, quickly established themselves as strong and reliable. In a rare fit of generosity, Swindon graced them with copper capped chimneys. They could regularly be seen handling coal trains in excess of 900 tons down the valleys, a rake of 60 empties up, normal passenger workings or heavily loaded excursion trains. *(LCGB)*

Above and opposite above: Merthyr High Street 'seen here 10 December 1947' opened on 2 November 1853. The overall roofing covered platforms 1 to 4. Platform 5 was outside this but had a platform face on either side, both with an arced canopy of equal length. The eastern face was much shorter with a sixth siding abutting the platform end. A similar canopy of the same length extended from the overall roof on platform 1 but no such facility existed on 3 or 4. Platforms 1 and 2 had a trailing crossover at the buffer stops, 3 and 4 did not. The overall roof was still extant in 1950 but before this time had lost its front (but not rear) fascia, much reducing the visual impact.

   Arrivals could only access platforms 1 and 2 but departures could be accommodated from all five. Merthyr Station Signal Box controlled the whole station area while Mardy Junction was next in advance giving access to the Engine Yard and the divergence from the Taff Vale main line towards the B&M/LNW Joint, RR/GW Joint, and GW (Vale of Neath). The very substantial Goods Yard (adjacent to the station) surprisingly had no headshunt and all shunting movements would need to occupy the Down Main Line. (*Great Western Trust*)

Opposite below: Pontypool Road looking North towards Hereford 27 July 1963. Before Birmingham New Street became the cross-roads of the UK network, the North & West (Crewe to Newport) was a major arterial route. At Pontypool Road, passenger services combined or split into a South Wales and a West of England portion, and the Kings were seen here long before Cardiff. (*P.J. Garland*)

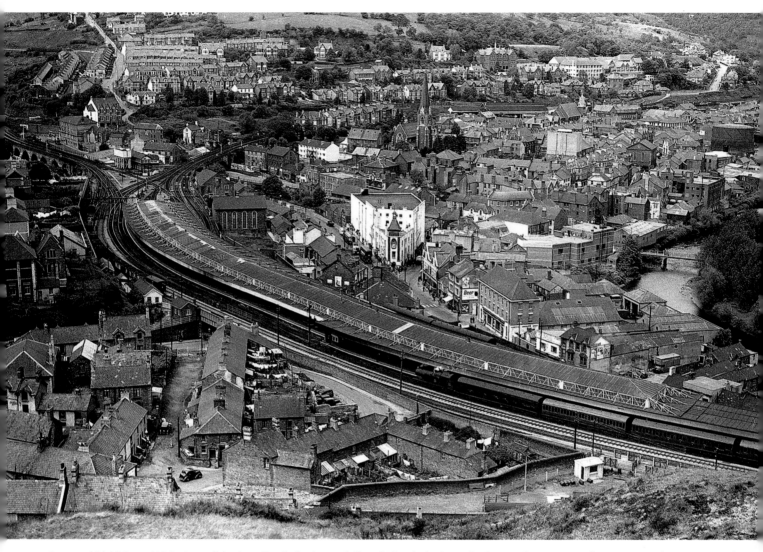

Pontypridd 12 June 1956. One of the bustling hubs, its multifaced island platform dealing with in excess of 10,000 people arriving and departing daily, together with many more changing from one valley service to another and over 100 passenger trains per day. Set on a right-hand curve, the station, situated on the lower slopes of a hill with the continued development of traffic, remained a two-track bottleneck until 1902 when the Taff Vale excavated the hillside and laid a double mineral line clear of the station.

With no room for further expansion, one of the most imaginative stations ever designed came into being. Up and Down platforms were replaced with one immense island platform 3,462ft long and 8,205sqyd surface with access from a booking hall below at street level.

The island has a unique combination of stepping and bays to give a total of seven platform faces. There were two bays at the Northern end for Aberdare, Nelson and Ynysybwl, with one at the south for Llantrisant and Cowbridge. Rebuilding in this form took from 1907 to 1912 to complete, the single storey station building finished in a glazed red brick beneath a single awning of no less than 7,370 square yards.

North of here, such passenger services threaded through the coal traffic of the Cynon, Taff and Rhondda Valleys which at one time amounted to over 17m tons annually. If it is assumed that this traffic was in trainloads of 60 x 10-ton wagons, a train of loaded coal or an empty return working passed Pontypridd every 8 minutes, day and night. (*D.K. Jones/Cresselley collection*)

The 48XX Class 0-4-2 tanks (renumbered 14xx in the autumn of 1946 to make way for oil-fired 2-8-0s) were difficult to pin down with only a brace at Fishguard and Pontypool Road sheds. However, 4871 was shedded from new in April 1936 at Llantrisant for working the Penygraig and Cowbridge services. In 1955, the British Transport Commission gave licence for the regions to adorn passenger engines with lined green livery. BR Green was not far removed from the GW's post 1928 Green and Swindon welcomed the edict with relish and included the diminutive 14XXs. The pose adopted here by 1471 at Llantrisant on 31 May 1958 seems to justify the decision. *(R.W.A. Jones/Online Transport Archive)*

June 1963 and 80133 on the 5.05pm from Swansea waits to return from Porthcawl at 6.32pm. The locomotive has been turned by means of a triangle that led from the outer platform and bordered the carriage sidings. Several of these magnificent machines had been transferred to Paxton Street for working over the Central Wales Line after electrification of the London, Tilbury and Southend Line. Only 80133 however explored other parts of South Wales and became something of a celebrity. *(F.K. Davies)*

Porthcawl, September 1962; a DMU forms the 6.55pm to Newport but the 6.32pm to Swansea has a more exotic charge in the form of Fowler 2-6-4T 42388. The former LNWR Shed at Swansea Paxton Street closed in August 1959 and its locomotives transferred to Swansea East Dock. From 12 June 1961, Swansea Landore was closed to steam, its remaining charges and associated services transferred to Neath (Court Sart) and Llanelli. Some contrivance by the respective shed foremen at East Dock and Neath must have occurred to give rise to this exclusive event. *(F.K. Davies)*

Taking advantage of one of the world's deepest natural harbours, several oil refineries were established around the Milford Haven and new rail terminals established. The first of these was the Esso Refinery at Herbrandston. 4928 *Gatacre Hall*, seen here working tender first, is about to join the main line at Herbrandston Junction with a modest load of ten oil tanks in the early days of this new traffic, 10 July 1962.

Three days later on 13 July, 6316 is in fine form as she heads up country with a more respectable load, having called at Haverfordwest to pick up traffic, and approaches Clarbeston Road.

The Taff Vale A Class was introduced in 1914 and conceived as the Taff's premier passenger engine. Fifty-eight in number, they were built by Hawthorn Leslie (30), Nasmyth Wilson (9), North British (6) and Vulcan Foundry (13). Seen here in original form is 414 (Vulcan Foundry) at Cardiff Queen Street in 1923, renumbered 404 in 1923 and finally 306 in 1946. All passed into BR ownership. *(LCGB H3532)*

They were rebuilt by the GW between 1926 and 1932. In this form they were handsome, powerful, extremely reliable and well liked with a good turn of speed. It is said they were preferred even to the 56s for passenger workings. The 23 rebuilt at Caerphilly and the first 9 at Swindon retained their round topped tanks then Swindon adopted square tops as seen on 381 (TV 159) at Ferry Road on 22 April 1953. (*Alan A. Jarvis 0116/Stephenson Locomotive Society*)

The last A to work a Passenger turn was 373 on Saturday 5 June 1957. 373 & 390 were condemned on 31 October 1957. Two hundred and forty-three of the 793 pre-grouping locos at 1923 (some 31 per cent) survived into BR ownership. In 1922, 1938 and 1947 the Newport, Neath & Cardiff Valleys Divisions together operated 44 per cent, 40 per cent and 37 per cent of the total GW locos. Here, 387 is captured in a splendid broadside at Cardiff East Dock shed in August 1956. (*Great Western Trust*)

The Taff Vale O4 Class was introduced in 1907. Forty-one in number, 36 were rebuilt by the GW; again like the Class As the Caerphilly rebuilds retained round topped tanks but those at Swindon square tops as seen on 211 at Cardiff General 27 August 1953. The last four members of the class were withdrawn in July 1955. (Alan A. Jarvis 0387/Stephenson Locomotive Society)

Amongst the best remembered of 0-6-2Ts for mineral working is the Rhymney R Class originating from 1907. The class comprised fifteen engines. A fine testimony to their original design is that they received little rebuilding and two (36/38) were the last pre-grouping engines to survive. 37 is shown here at Cathays yard 24 August 1947. The Locomotive Superintendent of the Rhymney Railway 1906-22 was C.T. Hurry Riches whose father T. Hurry Riches was the Locomotive Superintendent of the Taff Vale Railway 1873-1911. (Great Western Trust)

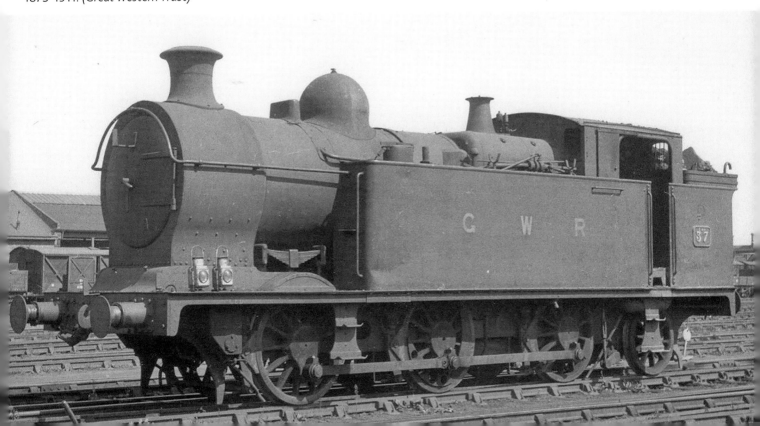

End of an era on Monday, 7 October 1957. Former Rhymney Railway R class Nos 38 & 36 are about to start their final journey from Cardiff East Dock shed to Swindon Works for condemnation. Their last week had been in revenue earning service working mineral traffic from the Rhymney valley. On the footplate of No 38 was Driver W. Harris who had been a young fireman when the locomotive arrived new in 1922 from Hudswell Clarke. The engines were stopped at Gloucester as No 36 needed attention to the safety valve before continuing their journey the following day. They were broken up by early November. These were the last two pre-grouping 0-6-2Ts in the South Wales Valleys. *(Great Western Trust)*

Caerphilly Works was enhanced under the GW to become the 'Swindon' of Wales and undertook heavy maintenance of all classes of locomotives. Despite an edict from Swindon, Caerphilly continued to outshop locomotives with Brass Domes and Safety valve covers. It also had a penchant for painting Reversing levers red, but this practice was soon dropped as, universally, red was the signal for danger. *(Great Western Trust)*

In this view of the main erecting shop, 4177 is undergoing repairs some time in 1958. *(R.W.A. Jones/ Online Transport Archive)*

Caerphilly being the largest castle in Britain may explain why the GW chose the name for the first member of the Castle class in 1923. However, the GW, ever diplomatic and recognising the recent inclusion into its fold of the Welsh Companies, also saw it as a token of homage. The Castles were at the forefront of Express Passenger Services until Western Region Dieselisation in 1962.

To discourage favouritism (or perhaps encourage bi-lingualism) the GW had a policy of not allocating engines with Welsh names to Welsh Sheds. So, 4073 'seen here outside the works in October 1959' would have been treated like a Royal visitor. It was also standard practice at English sheds not to replenish Welsh based engines with coal if working home. For this reason, at Paddington, rather than trek to Old Oak Common, incoming Welsh engines went to Ranelagh Bridge (adjacent to the station throat) purely for turning, watering and stabling until the return working. *(Great Western Trust)*

The 42XXs were built specifically for the short runs of heavy coal trains in South Wales. The Stock Market Crash of 1929 saw coal traffic dramatically fall so the decision was taken to rebuild 54 of them with extended coal carrying capacity for greater range and usefulness. This added 4ft to the frames, requiring the addition of a trailing wheel set, making them 2-8-2Ts. Weighing in at 92¾ tons, 7222 features here in Aberdare shed yard. With six tons of coal in the bunker, a round trip from Aberdare to Salisbury would be well within her range. 26 August 1964. *(D.K. Jones/ Cresselley Collection)*

Above left: A significant source for GW engine names

Above right: South Wales resorts. You cannot find any fault under the Trades Description Act.

Left: Porthcawl in 1829 was the first railway-served docks in the world. The opening of the Port Talbot Railway in 1897 destroyed Porthcawl's coal exporting trade within a few years. Faced with this, the GW successfully built up a tourist traffic making use of Porthcawl's wide beaches, the only sheltered sandy beaches between Barry Island and the Gower. However, Porthcawl never achieved the popularity of Barry. This was perhaps just as well considering its limited siding accommodation that could accommodate no more than fourteen sets of empty stock for the day.

In every decade from 1841 to 1910 at least two docks were opened. Not surprisingly, the GW 'seeing the advantages of dock ownership' entered the fray by way of purchase of local companies in the C19th, thus ensuring for itself the dubious honour of being the only owner of the only South Wales Dock to close (Porthcawl 1914) at a time when the coal export trade was nearly at its peak, Porthcawl being unable to handle larger vessels. Porthcawl Dock in 1895. *(courtesy of Porthcawl Museum)*

Cefn Coed Viaduct (Brecon & Merthyr Railway) '768ft' viewed 2 May 1964 from the footplate of 4555 which with 3690 worked an SLS special (the last train) from Merthyr to Brecon. *(P.J. Garland)*

Llanbradach Viaduct (Barry Railway) 2,400ft. Ranking amongst the greatest in South Wales, a tremendous structure with eleven lattice girders 162ft each resting on brick piers 125ft above the valley floor and carrying the Barry Railway with splendid arrogance across the Rhymney river from Glamorgan to Monmouthshire. It was demolished in 1937 after the peak of the South Wales Coal trade. (*Great Western Trust*)

Crumlin Viaduct (VoN) 1,658ft, with seven spans over the River Ebbw and three over the River Kendon. It cost £62,000 in 1853 and was opened 1 June 1857 with cannon firing alternately from either side of the valley throughout the day. Piers composed of tubular cast iron columns 12ft in diameter were braced with cross-struts built up in tiers, doing away with scaffolding. Each span was 130ft and 208ft above the valley floor. The viaduct featured in the 1966 film *Arabesque* starring Sophia Loren. Drivers said it had a pronounced tendency to swing sideways under the weight of a train like an Atlantic swell. Passengers changing trains between Crumlin HL & LL did so with a walk of some ¼ mile with an ascent or descent of 200ft at 1:6. An 84XX heads across the viaduct with a service from Neath to Pontypool Road 15 May 1964. (*Alan A. Jarvis 2774/Stephenson Locomotive Society*)

Above: A view from Crumlin Viaduct looking North with Navigation Colliery on the left, the Western Valley Line centre and a Red & White bus heading for Newport on the A4046 right. 21 March 1964. *(London Area Collection/Online Transport Archive)*

Right: Walnut Tree Viaduct (Barry Railway) 1,548ft, comprising seven steel lattice girder spans resting on massive masonry piers 120ft above the valley floor of the River Taff and the Taff Vale Main Line. The viaduct was demolished on 29 September 1969. An LNW G2A from Abergavenny or Tredegar crosses the Viaduct with a Barry Island Excursion in August 1955. *(Alan A. Jarvis 0675/ Stephenson Locomotive Society)*

Gelli Felin Viaduct (LNW), 312ft, in the Clydach Gorge between Abergavenny and Brynmawr on the MT&A. This view of the viaduct looking towards Abergavenny gives some idea of the terrain encountered by the LNW in reaching Merthyr as 6411 heads its modest train 28 August 1957. *(R.W.A. Jones/Online Transport Archive)*

Far left: Tenby was not a major day trip venue which was fortunate, having no siding capacity for stock.

Left: Easter Monday, 21 April 1930, a rugby match in the holy of holies (the Arms Park), option of an evening at the theatre before returning from Queen Street at 11pm with a 2¾ hour journey to and from Builth Wells. The Mid Wales signalmen would be on overtime and so everyone is happy.

The GW operated Steam Rail Motors from 1903 until 1935 ultimately with 99 in service. Seen here near Golden Hill Tunnel (one mile East of Pembroke) No. 68 forms the 3.28pm service to Whitland. *(Great Western Trust)*

The GW loved attaching odd vehicles to local services as seen behind No. 68 again here at Lamphey. Referred to as 'Tail Traffic,' the practice continued with Auto trains, Diesel Railcars and ultimately the Western Region with Diesel Multiple Units.

In 1907, the Rhymney procured two Steam Rail Motors, the locomotive built by Hudswell Clarke and the saloon by Cravens. Numbered 1 (recorded here) & 2, they lasted until 1910 and 1919. *(Great Western Trust)*

The Taff Vale first introduced a Steam Rail Motor in 1903. Subsequently raised to a total of 13, Numbers 8 to 13 were 3rd class only. One of these, No.11, is shown here. TV operation of SRMs lasted until 1920. *(Great Western Trust)*

Barry Railway Steam Rail Motor Nº2 built by the North British Locomotive Co. Supplied along with No. 1 in 1905, they were withdrawn in 1913. *(Great Western Trust)*

The GW owned no major ports in South Wales before 1922 and was therefore never a major exporter of coal up to this date. Its involvement in the Monmouthshire, Ely, Ogmore and Llynfi valleys was largely confined to the English market for coal. Thus, the GW concentrated on the long haul to inland markets in the Midlands, the South and Southwest. As a result, with two exceptions it saw no need to develop locos for the coal trade. The first was William Dean's Aberdare class, an outside framed 2-6-0 introduced in 1900 and so named for the preponderance of the class based at Aberdare. 2667 appropriately on shed at Aberdare 21 July 1935. (W.A. Camwell)

The second was Churchward's 42xx 2-8-0T introduced in 1910. The majority spent most of their lives in South Wales allocated to pedigree GW rather than pre-grouping sheds and for many it was the only home they knew. 4258 and 4235 are recorded at Newport Pill sometime in 1959. Regardless of the load, you never saw one of these lose their footing. (R.W.A. Jones/Online Transport Archive)

Three Cocks Junction, 46512 with a train from Moat Lane left and 46514 with a connecting service from Hereford right, 5 June 1962. The curious name of the junction was derived from the fifteenth century Three Cocks Inn, a coaching inn, still extant, which in turn took its name from the armorial bearings of former local landowners, the Williams family of Old Gwernyfed. To Railwaymen, it was referred to as 'Lucky Man Junction.' The Junction was where the Midland Railway (Hereford, Hay and Brecon Branch) from Hereford joined the Cambrian Railways (Mid Wales Line) from Moat Lane Junction (48¼ miles) to Talyllyn Junction. The station layout comprised of a large 'V' with lines converging from Hereford in the east with the Mid Wales from the north, then heading away south to Talyllyn Junction where trains diverged again for Brecon or the South Wales valleys. The first 29 chains of the Hereford line were Cambrian owned. The Midland had running powers from here to Talyllyn Junction and Brecon. The station layout was simple enough, Up and Down platforms for both the Cambrian and Midland lines. The station was situated within flat pastoral land and was approached on a wide leafy avenue, with the nearest settlement being Aberllynfi. Passenger facilities included a waiting room, ticket office and a refreshment room, all the amenities being housed in a single building which was situated centre of the V-shaped platform. Despite the refreshment room being licensed, remote from any hamlet and only four-minute connections between trains, it is difficult to comprehend who its patrons were. Three Cocks Signal Box was a Dutton & Co Type 1 Brick platform signal box measuring 24ft 8in x 11ft x 9ft which opened on 26 October 1890. Internally it was fitted out with a 40-lever frame facing the Cambrian main line, for ease of observation; the signalman had an all-round vision within the box. *(Alan A. Jarvis 2218/Stephenson Locomotive Society)*

Above: Three Cocks Junction and Cambrian 15 Class 896 heads the 9.55 Moat Lane to Brecon service on 11 September 1951. Swindon constructed a batch of LMS Ivatt Moguls in 1952 (46503-46527) to replace ageing Dean and Cambrian 0-6-0s in the Oswestry District. Of these, eight were based at Brecon and were programmed to work all the passenger services to Hereford and Moat Lane. Occasionally one could be found on the Brecon to Newport service. (*Great Western Trust*)

Opposite above: Unusually, the turntable at Brecon was adjacent to the station rather than part of the locomotive shed. Here 3661 is being turned in readiness for her return journey to Newport, 8 August 1962. It was standard practice in South Wales for tank engines to face chimney leading up the valley and bunker leading down (facilitating orientation in photographs). This, in concert with the gradient, ensured water in the boiler covered the firebox crown, preventing the fusible safety plug from melting. In the case of Newport-Brecon services however, the gradients were much the same in both directions and locomotives were turned at both ends of the line. There was more to be gained in facing the direction of travel by the driver and fireman than avoiding the arduous task of pushing the turntable.

   The station at Brecon had originating services to Hereford, Moat Lane, Neath and Newport. It consisted of a main platform with an adjacent East facing bay and an island platform which was reached by passengers having to cross the tracks as Brecon had no footbridge. (*Alan A. Jarvis 1477/Stephenson Locomotive Society*)

Opposite below: The Train Indicator recorded here at Talyllyn Junction reflects those odd moments when the rustic idyll was shattered by a burst of frenzied hustle and bustle, 7 July 1962. (*Alan A. Jarvis 1597/Stephenson Locomotive Society*)

Above: 8781 & 8787 slowing for the scheduled stop at Talybont with 20 Ammonia Tanks for Dowlais, 27 May 1959. If the load required, two Hereford engines worked throughout (with Hereford Crews) at this time. The schedule at Talybont of 2.36 to 2.46pm allowed the pilot to take water then transfer to the rear of the train for the attack of the Seven Mile Bank immediately ahead.

Ammonia production at the ICI Works, Dowlais commenced on 13 January 1940. The empty tanks arriving daily from Haverton Hill on Teesside and originally routed via Abergavenny onto the LNWR (MT&A). When freight services were withdrawn from this on 22 November 1954, the train was re-routed via Hereford (leaving at 12.35pm) through Three Cocks & Talyllyn Junctions. The Dowlais works were connected by a siding to the B&M Dowlais Branch at Ivor No. 1 Junction. (*D.S. Fish*)

Opposite above: Talybont on Usk and unusual passenger, 7 July 1962. The Seven Mile Bank is built along a shelf cut into the hillside on the eastern flank of Glyn Collwng. Climbing begins at Talybont where, because of sharp grades at either end of the platform, the passing loops were extended at each end in case drivers had difficulty controlling their trains. Immediately on leaving the station, there were 6½ miles of unrelenting slog at 1:38. Then, half a mile below Torpantau Tunnel, this eases to 1:68 so that southbound trains had to climb 925ft in 7 miles. Passenger trains were allowed 28 to 30 minutes to make the 7¼ mile climb from Talybont to Torpantau, freight trains 44 minutes and restricted to a length of 35 wagons. (*Alan A. Jarvis 1596/Stephenson Locomotive Society*)

Opposite below: Halfway up the Seven Mile bank was Pentir Rhiw with its signal box, loop and miniscule island platform. It was a beautiful setting, the reservoir occupying the flooded Glyn Collwng to the west of the line and the afforested slopes of Tor y Foel rising to the east. It was included in the B&M's 1909 timetable as a conditional stop. Pentir Rhiw was a passing place where the signalman looked after the loop and a funicular-like runaway siding that ran crazily up the mountainside. He also issued tickets from a window in the signal box. Here 3747 on full regulator raises the echoes in Glyn Collwng on the way up the Seven Mile Bank as she approaches Pentir Rhiw with the 12.10pm Brecon to Newport, Friday 7 September 1962. (*Mike Roach*)

The Barry Railway constructed several of its stations with four tracks to enable mineral trains to pass unimpeded by stopping passenger services. Southerndown Road in the Vale of Glamorgan demonstrates this generous approach as seen here on 12 July 1959. 'Road' in a station name gave an indication the place you intended to be was some distance away, in this case 4 miles. The main building was located on the Down platform to a design common to Rhoose, Gileston, Llantwit Major and Aberthaw. Footbridges at each of these were supplied by Lysaght & Co. and the signal boxes by Evans O'Donnell & Co. *(Great Western Trust)*

Further west, two quarries were served and the associated signal box bore the grand name of 'Duchy & Lancaster Quarries Signal Box'. In this rare view, 5609 heads a Vale of Glamorgan service from Bridgend to Barry in May 1954. *(R.W.A. Jones/Online Transport Archive)*

Any Gallery of South Wales would be incomplete without a portrait of the quintessential Sheep. Here at Llanharan on 4 June 1963, a flock is being herded across the main line. One hopes the lineside telephone has been used to seek the signalman's permission to do so, safely. *(Alan A. Jarvis 2322/Stephenson Locomotive Society)*

Waenavon Station (LNW) at 1,400ft above sea level was the highest station on the national network. Regular traffic ceased in 1953 and the line officially closed in June 1954. Seen here on 28 August 1957. *(R.W.A. Jones/Online Transport Archive)*

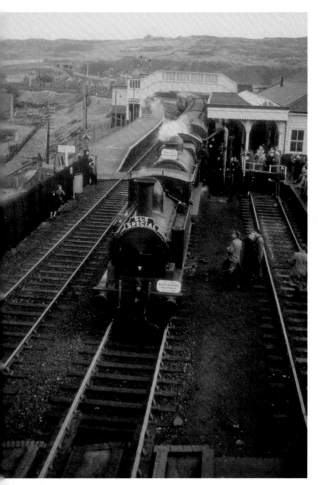

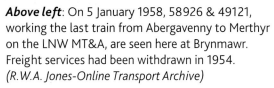

Above left: On 5 January 1958, 58926 & 49121, working the last train from Abergavenny to Merthyr on the LNW MT&A, are seen here at Brynmawr. Freight services had been withdrawn in 1954. (R.W.A. Jones-Online Transport Archive)

Above right: Getting ready for the special, Webb Coal Tank 58926 is recorded in spruced condition at Abergavenny. Here several of these locomotives were to be found along with Tredegar and Swansea Paxton Street sheds. The Rhymney Railway afforded the LNW running powers to Cardiff Docks and a Coal Tank was also shedded at Cardiff East Dock for shunting purposes. 58926, built at Crewe in 1888, fortunately has passed into preservation. (R.W.A. Jones/Online Transport Archive)

Right: Heading for Merthyr, a two car Auto train with a 64XX approaches the twin bore Gelli Felin Tunnel. The view gives some idea of the construction and operational challenges the MT&A presented, little wonder freight services were withdrawn in 1953 and complete closure soon after this photograph was taken, 30 November 1957.

9662 of Ebbw Junction Shed appears to be having some difficulty getting an Up Class K train of pit props on the move from the sidings at Park Junction, Monday 23 August 1954. The section from Park Junction to Bassaleg Junction was known as the Golden Mile, so called because of the tolls originally levied by Lord Tredegar for traversing his land. *(D.K. Jones/Cresselley Collection)*

Aberbeeg was the nucleus of the Western Valleys with an extensive yard and locomotive shed. It was the limit of a four-track railway virtually all the way from Park Junction with a fork for Abertillery and Brynmawr in the Ebbw Fach or Ebbw Vale in the Ebbw Fawr. Threading its way through the junction is 5206 with a train of empty mineral wagons bound for Rose Heyworth colliery. On the smokebox door is the 86H Shedplate, the BR designation for Aberbeeg Shed, and Target Disc A3 on the right-hand lamp bracket denoting duty 3 of Aberbeeg. Rose Heyworth colliery was one of four in the South Wales coalfield with a feminine name, the others being Lady Windsor at Ynysybwl, Lady Margaret at Treherbert and Lady Lewis at Ynyshir. *(R.W.A. Jones/Online Transport Archive)*

Dowlais Top on the B&M was the watershed between a continuous climb from Newport soon to be followed by a descent all the way to Brecon or vice versa and also marked the boundary between industrial and rural South Wales. The location was on an exposed ridge of barren, windswept, uninhabited moorland where the signal box stood sentinel over a level crossing. 9616 gets ready to depart with the 8.03 Newport to Brecon service in 1958. *(Marcus Eavis/ Online Transport Archive)*

Talyllyn Tunnel (B&M) 674yds, was opened in 1816 and is the oldest railway tunnel in the world. Viewed from the platform looking towards Brecon, 18 May 1959. *(Alan A. Jarvis 0068/Stephenson Locomotive Society)*

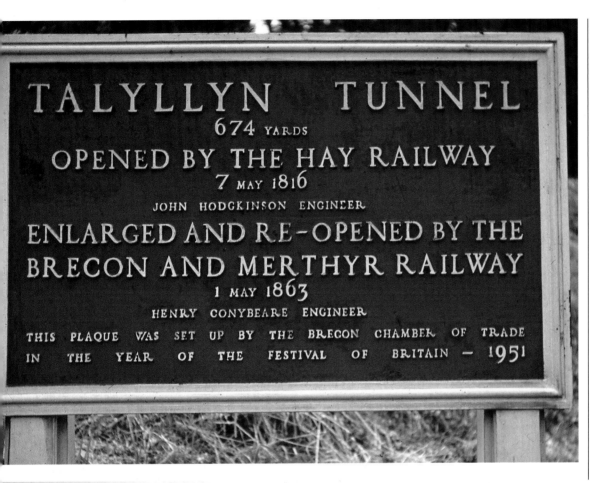

TALYLLYN TUNNEL
674 YARDS
OPENED BY THE HAY RAILWAY
7 MAY 1816
JOHN HODGKINSON ENGINEER
ENLARGED AND RE-OPENED BY THE
BRECON AND MERTHYR RAILWAY
1 MAY 1863
HENRY CONYBEARE ENGINEER
THIS PLAQUE WAS SET UP BY THE BRECON CHAMBER OF TRADE
IN THE YEAR OF THE FESTIVAL OF BRITAIN – 1951

Adjacent to the platform seen in the previous image, a plaque to commemorate its heritage was erected in 1951 at the time of the Festival of Britain. 13 June 1959. *(Alan A. Jarvis 0136/Stephenson Locomotive Society)*

Emerging from the south portal and into Torpantau station on 13 June 1959 is 9776 with a Goods to Merthyr. *(Alan A. Jarvis 0130/Stephenson Locomotive Society)*

The northern portal of Summit Tunnel is seen here as 8766 'with the 12.10pm Brecon to Newport' is about to enter. Summit Tunnel, or incorrectly referred to as Torpantau Tunnel (B&M) 660yds, at 1,313ft above sea level is the highest tunnel in Britain. Monday 18 May 1959. *(Alan A. Jarvis 0081/Stephenson Locomotive Society)*

The Capstone from the Rhondda Tunnel is now to be found at the Miners' Museum at Afan Argoed near Cynonville. The Rhondda Tunnel (R&SBR) was 3,443 yards and completed in July 1890 at the cost in its construction of 5 fatalities. There is an ambitious plan to reopen it as a cycleway. *(Author's Collection)*

Above: Rhondda Tunnel North portal at Blaenycwm 7 August 1965. Despite its claim to fame as the longest tunnel within Wales, neither portal could be described as prestigious. To railwaymen, it was always a 'wet' tunnel. *(Author's collection)*

Left: Rhondda Tunnel South portal with a train from Neath to Treherbert headed by a 94XX approaching from Blaengwynfi. 13 May 1957.

Below: To work the South Wales Valleys was to work on steep gradients which generated local practices not applicable elsewhere on the system. Pantywaun Halt (B&M) was a case in point. Situated on a 1:37 between Fochriw and Dowlais Top, drivers of Up trains would come up the climb from Fochriw at full regulator until the engine was alongside the platform ramp and then quickly shut off steam. The train would then come to a halt within the platform barely the length of the train. Then and only then would the brakes be applied, not to stop the train but to hold it on the gradient. Pantywaun Halt 5615 11.35am SO Bargoed to Dowlais Central Workmen's service 24 May 1958 *(Great Western Trust)*

A view of the line from Merthyr below left as we approach Pontsticill Junction Monday 24 December 1962. *(Alan A. Jarvis 2014/Stephenson Locomotive Society)*

Looking west from the station at Pontsticill Junction 18 May 1959. What an idyllic place to work! *(Alan A. Jarvis 0067/Stephenson Locomotive Society)*

Between Caerphilly and Machen, the tracks were owned by the B&M but the passenger services worked by the RR, A(N&SW)D&R or GW. To ease the gradient for Eastbound trains, the Up and Down Lines were separated into two single lines on opposite sides of the valley for about 1½ miles. Uniquely, the two single lines each had a passenger halt, Fountain Bridge Halt in Monmouthshire, served by trains to Newport. 5 August 1963. (Garth Tilt)

Whilst Waterloo Halt in Glamorgan was served by trains to Caerphilly. 5 August 1963. (Garth Tilt)

The LNW only dominated in the Sirhowy Valley, even then only as far as Nine Mile Point where it was obliged to make an end on junction with the GW and the running powers only allowed access to Newport for its passenger services. As a result, Sirhowy Coal traffic was routed by means of Bird in Hand Jcn, Pontllanfraith, Ystrad Mynach and thence to Cardiff in conjunction with the RR or to Newport by the A(N&SW)D&R via Machen and Bassaleg. Here, Nine Mile Point is viewed from No. 2 SB with 41204 heading the 1.10pm Newport to Tredegar while 40171 waits to work a Northbound Miners' service, August 1952. *(A.C. Sterndale)*

At Brynmawr 7840 is seen with the 5.20pm from Ebbw Vale (High Level) on 20 September 1947. Operation of the services over the short branches of the MT&A were in the best traditions of complex relationships of South Wales Railways. Of the branches, only that from Brynmawr to Ebbw Vale was worked by the LNW. The others were operated by the GW or RR from either Cardiff or Newport. *(W.A. Camwell)*

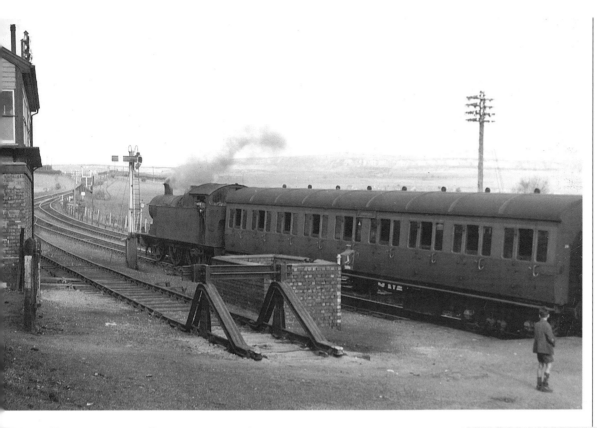

Here at Rhymney Bridge, having traversed Rhymney and for the final stretch LNW metals, a service from Cardiff Queen Street is worked by a former Taff Vale A Class. 7 May 1949. *(Lens of Sutton)*

Even the Sirhowy had been 'westernised' before its demise. Nantybwch is seen here with panniers 3634 and 8711 on the last day of service. 11 June 1960. *(M.B. Warburton/ Stephenson Locomotive Society)*

Nevertheless, despite efforts to mask the origins of what was referred to as the 'penetrating lines' most had some means of identifying their ancestry, in this case Nantybwch (LNW) in 1958. Failing to eradicate the heritage, closure was the solution. *(D.K. Jones/Cresselley Collection)*

To most people, South Wales conjures up a picture of terraced houses on slopes interspersed by areas of heavy industry. This view of Victoria (Ebbw Vale) in April 1962 features both with two blast furnaces of the Richard Thomas & Baldwin Steel Works. Coal and metals were the foundation on which the intense rail network in this area was developed. Freight was the priority and in 1976, one in every six wagons was to be found in South Wales. *(D.K. Jones/Cresselley Collection)*

However, few realise that amongst the industrialisation, nature can be found at its best as this sylvan setting attests. Blackmill with 5524 in Auto mode working a Nantymoel to Bridgend service Saturday 3 May 1958 Sadly, this was the last day of passenger services on the Ogmore Branch. *(D.K. Jones/Cresselley Collection)*

PENRHOS

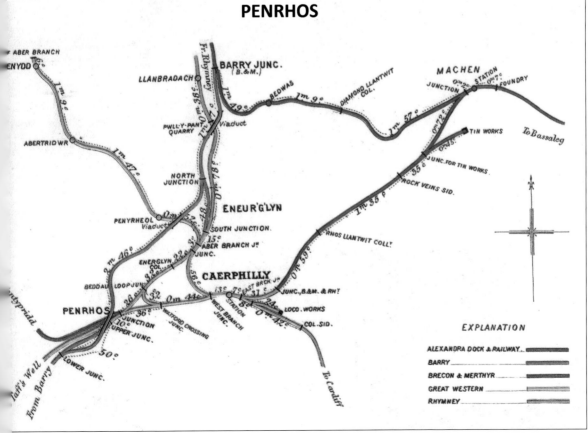

A picture paints a thousand words. The complexity of Penrhos Junction is depicted here identifying the ownership of lines.

Penrhos Jcn looking West. The section from Penrhos Lower Jcn to North Jcn was decommissioned in 1926 but a bridge is seen still in place (above the 56XX) in this view dated 1935. *(Great Western Trust)*

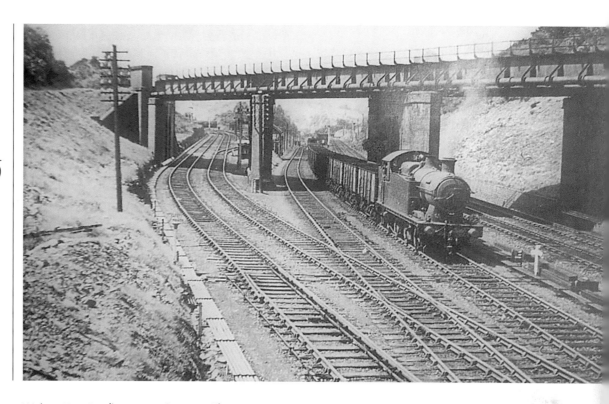

Most trains coming from Walnut Tree Jcn (known as the Big Hill) required a banker; an 875X fulfilling the role here on 27 August 1964 and just dropping away from the train. A loaded train passes on the Down Line. It was on one such occasion, the Divisional Trains Inspector Tom Holloway presented the author with a gradient compass (a tin and ball bearing). *(Alan A. Jarvis 2987/Stephenson Locomotive Society)*

5627 passing through Taffs Well Station bunker first with a Down Class J mineral train. Barry workings were not too common on this stretch of line as most Down freights used the Treforest Junction -Cadoxton route so possibly 5627 was on loan to another shed at this time. Behind the train can be seen 'the big hill' up to Penrhos Junction and Caerphilly. Friday 10 June 1955. *(D.K. Jones/Cresselley Collection)*

6612 rounding the curve at what was known amongst railwaymen as 'Knacker's Point,' high above Taffs Well, with the Y13 9.45am Walnut Tree West-Aber Junction Class K freight. Another mineral train can be seen on the valley floor. Saturday 16 June 1955. *(D.K. Jones/Cresselley Collection)*

This 1962 view of the frontage is much the same today except the fact Cardiff General became Cardiff Central in 1973. In 1956 Cardiff was invested as the capital of the Principality and hosted the Commonwealth games; difficult to imagine that at the turn of the nineteenth century, Merthyr then was much larger with a population of 75,000. Cardiff was served by six railways: GW, LNW, Taff, Barry, Rhymney and Cardiff. *(Author's collection)*

The short Riverside Branch in Cardiff was owned by the GW, but the passenger services worked by the Taff Vale and Barry Railway. Seen here is the terminus at Clarence Road and 6438 with target JB working the 5.31pm Clarence Road to Pontypridd on 2 May 1959. For the purposes of identification, particularly signalmen, most passenger and freight trains in the Cardiff and Newport districts carried white discs mounted on a leading lamp bracket. These were stencilled with two or three digits, the first denoting the depot (in this case, J for Abercynon) and then letter(s) for a passenger turn and figures for goods and mineral trains. These would be cross-referenced with their respective programmes in the Service Timetables. Known as 'Target boards,' they were not generally used in the Neath district. *(R.W.A. Jones/ Online Transport Archive)*

Gateway to the Cardiff Valleys and the busiest station is Cardiff Queen Street. The frontage, seen here, was the headquarters of the Taff Vale Railway which were built in 1887 but demolished in 1973. 5 March 1957. *(Great Western Trust)*

Virtually alongside the Taff Vale, Queen Street station was the Rhymney Railway's Cardiff Parade. This was closed in 1926 when the GW enlarged the facilities at Queen Street. This June 1922 view is looking North and over the fence, the neighbour (TVR). *(D.K. Jones/ Cresselley Collection)*

Cornelius Lundie was born in Kelso in 1815. He was Traffic Manager of the Blythe & Tyne Railway when in 1863, at the age of 48, he came to Cardiff as General Manager of the Rhymney Railway. In addition to being General Manager, he also assumed the role of Chief Engineer and Locomotive Superintendent. At the end of 1904, being 89 years of age, he was persuaded to take lighter duties and became Consultant Director. In the annals of the Barry Railway, in its quest to further infiltrate the Coalfield and appropriate traffic from neighbouring railways, this grand old man of the Welsh railways gave evidence before a Parliamentary Committee of 1907 at the age of 92. He died on 12 February 1908 aged 93.

Above: Stations at smaller locations were still regarded as assets for the community and their designs commensurate with this principle. Llwynypia (TVR) in the Rhondda Valley 1960. *(D.K. Jones/Cresselley Collection)*

Opposite above: Rhoose (BR) in the Vale of Glamorgan 1963. *(Great Western Trust)*

Opposite below: The Up side station building at Chepstow owes its architectural design to the South Wales Railway (progeny of the GW). Built 1850, the building together with that at Bridgend have survived. April 1975. *(D.K. Jones/Cresselley Collection)*

The rivalry and complexity of the South Wales network resulted in many towns having more than one station. Aberdare is a case in point. The Taff Vale facility viewed here with 9777 in GW livery with 'W' suffix under the numberplate waits with the 11.2am to Abercynon 28 March 1963. The station was re-named Aberdare Low Level by the GW in 1923. *(D.K. Jones/Cresselley Collection)*

The GW station in Aberdare on the Vale of Neath line was, in 1923, re-named High Level and viewed here just before that time in 1922. The layout was restricted, being hemmed in by the River Cynon and the Taff Vale facilities, hence the staggered platforms. The Vale of Neath entered the GW fold in 1863. It was the GW's second arterial route in South Wales running from Pontypool Road to Neath General, a distance of 41¾ miles. With nineteen station stops the average journey time was two hours but strategically, had seventeen junctions linking it to most of the North/South Valley lines. Even more significantly, four tunnels (Glyn 280yds, Bryn 398yds, Quakers Yard 703yds, Pencaedrain 526yds) and seven viaducts (Neath 68yds, Dulais 73yds, Pontwalby 65yds, Quakers Yard 170yds, Treharris 78yds, Hengoed 299yds and Crumlin 550yds). *(D.K. Jones/Cresselley Collection)*

Some stations served working establishments rather than communities and Cefn Coed Colliery Halt (between Crynant and Cilfrew N&B), recorded in the 1950s, is an example. *(D.K. Jones/ Cresselley Collection)*

In the middle of nowhere, Cefn Coed Colliery Halt and 9621 approaches with the 1.00pm Colbren to Neath workmen's service on 6 October 1962. *(Alan A. Jarvis 1965/Stephenson Locomotive Society)*

Some stations were gateways to fun and Barry Island must rate as the South Wales classic, viewed here in 1922. *(D.K. Jones/Cresselley Collection)*

Barry Island handled 50,000 people at Summer weekends and operationally, return excursions departed at a rate of one every five minutes for an evening period extending up to four hours. Here 5649 & 9424 head the 6.30pm Cardiff Queen Street and 6.45pm Newport respectively whilst a rare visit from 1025 *County of Radnor* returns at 6.35pm to Tyseley on August Bank Holiday 6 August 1961. *(courtesy of John Hodge)*

On the same day, 5790 & 3706 wait to depart for Brecon. *(courtesy of John Hodge)*

For many years Diesel Railcar No. 4 'based at Landore' was to be found working the Morriston branch. Here she is seen at Swansea High Street in 1955. *(Leo Sullivan/Online Transport Archive)*

Some of the later 'Razor Edge' railcars were designed to work in pairs with a conventional coach sandwiched between. A regular Cardiff - Birmingham service, with miniature buffet, was introduced with this feature becoming so successful the service had to revert to traditional loco-hauled trains. DRCs 33 & 38 are featured here approaching Birmingham in 1955 although unlikely to be a Cardiff service at this time.

Another service in South Wales operated by DRCs was that between Pontypool Road and Monmouth where we see No. 30 heading for Pontypool Road with an Auto service for Chepstow alongside. Friday 28 August 1953. *(Alan A. Jarvis 0395/Stephenson Locomotive Society)*

On the same day, we see DRC No. 30 again in the North Bay at Pontypool Road on Friday 28 August 1953. *(Alan A. Jarvis 0389/Stephenson Locomotive Society)*

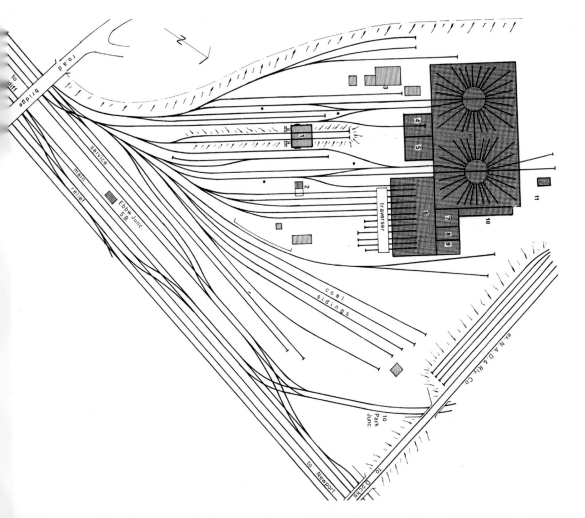

To maintain and operate the network, South Wales boasted some 60 engine sheds in 1922. Ebbw Junction was the second largest on the GW after Old Oak Common, Paddington. The layout is shown here. *(courtesy of E. Lyons)*

The LMS loco maintenance organisation differed from that of the GW most fundamentally in the way individual depots were regarded. Canton GW shed was subordinate to Ebbw Jcn only 14 miles distant but was equipped with modern machinery to carry out every repair and examination on its own allocation of locos. The only occasion they went elsewhere was for programmed overhaul at main works.

This feature was common to most GW sheds of any reasonable size, they were each entirely responsible for the maintenance of their own locos and every shed was staffed and equipped accordingly. Symptoms of the concentration depot syndrome were never manifest on the GW.

Instead of using the term District, a cluster of GW depots was called a Division and its overlord a Divisional Locomotive and Carriage & Wagon Superintendent responsible for every wheel that turned with a locomotive and a C&W specialist as his assistants. GW Divisional HQs offices were not part of the parent depot buildings as were the LMS District HQs, usually the GW provided Divisional office accommodation away from a loco shed and there was no parent depot in the LMS sense. The size of the facilities at Ebbw Junction Shed can be seen here when new in 1915. Its factory on the far right.

Ebbw Shed. *(Great Western Trust)*

Canton was host to all the celebrities, the cast of which was extended in September 1960 when six Kings, ousted from their West of England stomping ground, were given 86C Shedplates. 6018 *King Henry VI* and 6028 *King George VI* stand outside the Shed in April 1962. All thirty Kings were withdrawn in 1962. Because of their wide cylinders and the curvature of the Down Platform at Bridgend they were not allowed West of Cardiff. Ironically, 6023 & 6024 were sold for scrap to Thomas Ward at Briton Ferry, the restriction recalled and both were diverted to Woodhams Barry, the rest is history. *(Alan A. Jarvis 1323/Stephenson Locomotive Society)*

A veritable line up on Canton Shed; 6023 *King Edward II*, 7813 *Freshford Manor*, 5061 *Earl of Birkenhead* and 5903 *Keele Hall*, Canton, February 1962 *(Alan A. Jarvis 1185/Stephenson Locomotive Society)*

Missing from the foregoing family album. Without exception, every Western driver would sing praises for the 68XX Granges. The shed is bare except for 6860 *Aberporth Grange* and 6853 *Morehampton Grange* on 9 September 1962. The steam allocation was being transferred to Cardiff East Dock in preparation for diesel engine maintenance and Canton closed as a steam shed on 14 September 1962. *(Alan A. Jarvis 1839A/Stephenson Locomotive Society)*

On the WR the Britannias only found great favour at Canton possibly because the Top Link had been nurtured on the 'Saints'. It was said a 2 x cylinder engine was softer than a 4 x cylinder. Nevertheless, some fine performances were achieved on the main line with these machines. 70024 *Vulcan* at Cardiff General with the 'Red Dragon' 10am to Paddington 9 May 1961.

On 8 June 1963 at St Brides, 48706 heads for home from Severn Tunnel Junction with a heavy freight. Ostensibly for freight work on the Central Wales line, with an allocation of these machines at Llanelly, they could sometimes be found on the South Wales Main Line. In the right background is Newport's iconic transporter bridge, one of only eight worldwide. It is the oldest (1906) and largest of the three to be found in Britain. There was a maxim at Ebbw Junction Shed that if the traincrew saw the bridge, they'd want relief and if they couldn't, you never knew when you'd get them back again. *(Alan A. Jarvis 2345/Stephenson Locomotive Society)*

Pwllyrhebog incline on 4 May 1951. To serve the Clydach Vale Collieries, the line was worked by three specially designed Class H 0-6-0 tanks which, by a rope worked system, were assisted up the incline from the Junction just North of Tonypandy & Trealaw where for the first ¾ mile the gradient was 1:13. *(H.C. Casserley)*

The Pwllyrhebog branch was closed from 1 July 1951 and the three locomotives sold to the NCB. 193 was then based at Caerphilly Tar Works and is recorded here on 12 May 1956. Although little used in later years the locomotive was not condemned until January 1960. *(R.W.A. Jones/Online Transport Archive)*

Lying on the valley floor, Aberbeeg Shed was a standard Churchward straight shed opened in 1919, located ½ mile south of the station. *(Great Western Trust)*

Aberbeeg was home to around 37 tank engines. This being the case, like most of the valley sheds it had no turntable and when the first eight of the Standard 9F 2-10-0s were introduced in 1954, primarily to work Iron ore trains from Newport Docks, tender first running back to Newport was the order of the day. *(Great Western Trust)*

Nestled in something of a bowl was Duffryn Yard Shed known to its staff as Suffrin Yard. To reach the GW main line at Port Talbot General, a circuitous route of almost two miles was necessary, literally boxing the compass in the process. Lurking in the left-hand corner is former B&M 0-6-2T No. 428 on 29 August 1948. *(Great Western Trust)*

Duffryn Yard March 1961 with a more representative display of its steeds. Duffryn No. 1 Signal Box gives access to the PTR Main Line towards Bryn and Maesteg (Neath Road) or with a reversal, to Aberavon Town (R&SBR), Port Talbot Central (PTR) and Port Talbot General (GW). *(Alan A. Jarvis 0886/Stephenson Locomotive Society)*

Duffryn Yard Breakdown Train resplendent in red. March 1961. *(Alan A. Jarvis 0886A/Stephenson Locomotive Society)*

An alternative exit from Duffryn Yard was southwards towards Copper Works Junction and the Docks by means of Duffryn Junction No. 3 and Doctor's Level Crossing seen here. (*Great Western Trust*)

Canton's favourite (Saint class) was 2906 *Lady of Lynn*, built in May 1906 and the last example to work from a South Wales shed, was officially condemned on 16 August 1952. She remained alongside the southern wall of the straight shed until the 28th where during this period, under the orders of the shed foreman, 2906 was polished. She left South Wales still revenue earning, resplendent at the head of the 6.25am Cardiff to Moreton Cutting Goods before returning light engine to Swindon for scrapping. 2906 *Lady of Lynn* is captured here at Bridgend working the 10.10am Carmarthen to Gloucester on 10 April 1948. (*P. Pescod*)

Above: In 1937 the Milk Marketing Board established a processing factory at Pont Llanio (on the Carmarthen to Aberystwyth line) and in 1951, another at Felin Fach on the Lampeter to Aberayron branch. Cardiganshire was producing around 56,000 gallons daily. The milk traffic from both Pont Llanio and Felin Fach was conveyed by rail to Carmarthen for connection into the main line services which started at Whitland or Carmarthen. 25 June 1964 sees 7804 *Baydon Manor* near Conwil with the 10.35am Carmarthen to Aberystwyth passenger and includes a raft of empty milk tanks. These will be detached at Lampeter for forwarding to Felin Fach or else detached and shunted by 7804 into the adjacent Dairy Siding at Pont Llanio.

Right: On 13 November 1963, having collected the empties that have been left at Lampeter, 7439 positions them alongside the Green Grove Dairy at Felin Fach for loading.

Wagon label (Milk) from Felin Fach.

All four pre-Nationalisation companies carried milk traffic with the GWR having the largest share. The quantity moved by rail in 1929 was 230 million gallons. Here on 22 August 1962, undertaking preparatory work for the main line departures, 1613 is seen shunting at Whitland. In addition to the two milk tanks are the passenger train brakevans, the foremost 'No. 116' dating from 1934 branded Whitland and Kensington Milk. The other is a Hawksworth designed example built in 1949 easily discernible from all other coaching stock by their distinctive elliptical roof. Milk for processing at the two dairies at Whitland was brought in by road tanker.

Above: Seen 9 July 1962 departing Carmarthen is 5027 *Farleigh Castle* with the 6.45pm Milk to Kensington. The late 1920s saw the introduction of insulated 3,000-gallon rail tanks, the chassis owned by the railway and the tank by the milk company, some being of the roll on/roll off variety to facilitate transfer to and from road. All were vacuum braked and loaded with 3,000 gallons, weighing 35 tons. This and the need for speed required haulage by passenger class engines.

Opposite above: Passing through Ferryside on 9 July 1962 is 4081 *Warwick Castle* with 18 tanks plus passenger brakevan weighing in at 560 tons forming the 3.50pm Whitland to Kensington Milk. By the 1950s, four trains per day were scheduled Mon-Sat, three from Whitland and one from Carmarthen, all to Kensington where connections were made for the final destinations:

Whitland 3.50pm changing engines at Felin Fran on the Swansea District Line to a Swindon Castle off the 1am Paddington to Cardiff and 7.30am Cardiff to Swansea.

Whitland 5.15pm (if required) and Whitland 8.30pm both worked by Landore Castles to Swansea or Cardiff and thence Swindon or Canton Castles or Britannias (in the 1950s and early 60s).

Carmarthen 6.45pm: a Carmarthen or Old Oak Common engine throughout on alternate days. Loaded with tanks from Ffairfach, Llangadog and Pont Llanio as well as Carmarthen.

On Sundays four trains were also scheduled; from Whitland at 4.10pm, 5.25pm, 6.25pm, and from Carmarthen at 9.10pm.

With the 3.50pm Whitland to Kensington Milk, 5064 *Bishop's Castle* (SDN) rushes through Briton Ferry on 1 September 1961. The GWR also used twin-tank milk wagons so that different types of milk might be carried on the same wagon in lesser quantity. One of these is seen behind the locomotive tender. In addition to the Kensington traffic, a 4.45am Neath to Aberdare conveyed milk tanks from Ffairfach plus a brakevan which returned at 7.5am to Neath, the milk tanks from Aberdare being collected later in the day by the 3.50pm Pontypool Road to Neath. (*John Hodge*)

5000 *Launceston Castle* and 5023 *Brecon Castle* (both Swindon engines), after crew changes, set off from Canton with the 3.50pm Whitland to Kensington Milk Tuesday 28 April 1959. Double Heading was exceptional on the GW so there must have been a substantial load in tow. (*John Hodge*)

A small dairy existed at Marshfield. Empty milk tanks were supplied in the afternoon and loaded ones removed to/from Cardiff Canton. Here 9437 collects the day's milk output on 18 August 1963. (*Alan A. Jarvis 2487/Stephenson Locomotive Society*)

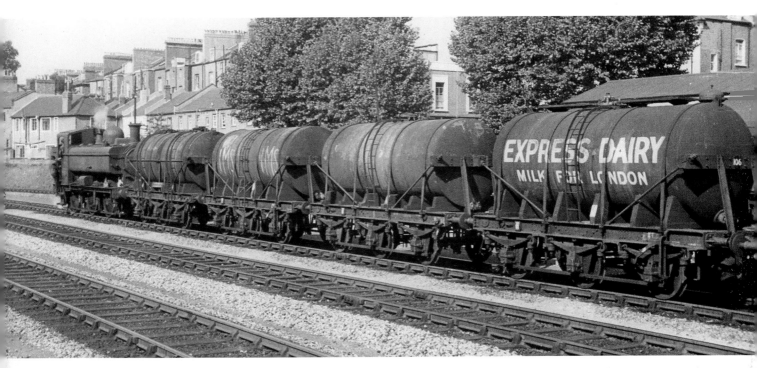

Journey's end. At Kensington Olympia, a pannier tank berths loaded milk tanks for discharging. Another of the twin tanks is next to the engine. Empty tanks were cleaned at either Carmarthen or Whitland milk depots and returned by:

10.35am Kensington to Neyland worked from Cardiff by a high-mileage Canton Castle or Britannia through to Neyland, returning next day with the 3.50pm Milford Haven Fish. It also conveyed empty Fish Vans to Neyland and Gas-Heated Brakevan 116 or 200 for the return Whitland Milk trains.

7.20pm (SX) 7.55pm (SO) Wood Lane to Whitland conveyed empty milk tanks for Ffairfach, Llangadog, Carmarthen, Pont Llanio and Whitland with Brakevan 79 or 187 which formed the 6.45pm to Kensington next day.

4.30pm Grimsby to Whitland mainly for fish traffic, with the vans continuing on to Neyland after being emptied but also conveyed some empty milk tanks.

1.15am (MO if Required) Swindon to Whitland delivered any surplus vans which had been worked into Swindon on Sundays, other tankers being conveyed on Parcels or Class 2 passenger services as tail traffic.

Chapel of Ease Crossing Signal Box (at the North end of Dyffryn yard) in March 1961. A chapel of ease is an Anglican (Church in Wales) church, built within the bounds of a parish for the attendance of those who cannot reach the parish church conveniently.

Holy Cross Church, Port Talbot, also known locally as the 'Chapel of Ease', was built in 1827 on land given by C.R.M. Talbot at Tonygroes as a chapel of ease to the then parish church which was at Margam over 2 miles away. After completion of St Theodore on Talbot Road in 1897, it was retained as a subsidiary and mainly used for Sunday Schools. It was closed formally in 2008 and declared redundant. Prior to the building of the M4 motorway flyover through the centre of the town in the 1960s, it was in the centre of a residential area but is now dominated by junction 40 of the motorway. (*Alan A. Jarvis 0887/Stephenson Locomotive Society*)

From the sublime to the ridiculous. Pontypool Road Station South Signal Box 'in June 1972' stands sentinel to the complexity that once existed at this location and gateway to the Vale of Neath, the GW's other East/West arterial route. The box had a frame of 155 levers. Pontypool boasted a confetti of stations; Pontypool Road, Clarence Street, Blaendare Road, Crane Street and to add to the Booking Office Clerk's nightmare, Lower Pontnewydd, Upper Pontnewydd and Pontnewynydd. (D.K. Jones/Cresselley Collection)

Abercwmboi Signal Box in 1963 still reflects its McKenzie & Holland design. With the exception of the Barry Railway, most of the South Wales companies purchased their signalling equipment from this company. (D.K. Jones/Cresselley Collection)

Meanwhile, Drope Signal Box was a product of Evans O'Donnell much favoured by the Barry Railway. Recorded in April 1962 with its original blue enamel nameplate. *(Alan A. Jarvis 1332/Stephenson Locomotive Society)*

Llangynwyd station and passing loop were situated in a cutting located about half-way between Bridgend and Abergwynfi. The signal box was just to the north of the Up-side platform. Llangynwyd was regularly timetabled for trains in opposite directions to pass one another. With single line sections either side of the station, the designated tokens needed to be surrendered and issued for both trains. The rules mandate that one train must come to a stand within a passing loop before the second is authorised to enter. Furthermore, from a practical point of view when exchanging tokens, it is last in first out and priority at Llangynwyd was given to Down Trains to avoid bringing them to a stand outside the station on the modestly rising gradient.

To facilitate the exchange here, auxiliary token exchange apparatus was provided. Even rarer however was a footbridge as seen in this view on 23 September 1963, extending from the box over the two running lines purely for use by the signalman to enable him to cross to the Down line when the Up line was already occupied in order to exchange tokens. The signal box was one of the smallest, the frame consisted of just 13 levers. *(P.J. Garland)*

Block-bells tinkle in the signal box and behind the open sliding windows can be seen the sudden movement of the signalman. More bells follow, levers clatter and lineside wires rustle; the Down-Home signal drops with a clatter and bounce. For a few minutes quiet descends again and then the sharp cry of a Swindon whistle sounds in the distance quickly followed by the scurrying silhouette of the branch train as it comes into sight half a mile away through the arch of the stone bridge. The faint rumble fades then grows into the unmistakeable bark of a '55' as the train re-appears end-on along the approach to the station. 5545 is sandwiched between one Auto-trailer fore and two aft.

As the train comes to a stand at the platform, the fireman leans out of the cab handing the Tondu North token to the signalman. By means of the bridge the signalman then returns to the box. There is a brief sound of opening and shutting doors as two or three passengers alight as another series of bell ringing occurs. The signalman taps 'Train Out of Section', inserts the token into the token instrument and secures 'Is Line Clear' from Tondu North for the Up train, the Down Home is returned to on, the south end loop points changed and the Up Starter pulled off.

The high bunker and cab roof of a Pannier lurch as she takes the loop points from the opposite direction with another train of three coaches but this time in conventional formation with the loco at the front, bunker leading in proper South Wales fashion. Meanwhile, the signalman re-emerges from his box, sedately descends the long flight of stairs and stands at their foot expectantly awaiting the Up train's arrival. The fireman leans out of the cab with his left hand held at right angles to his chest and his right hand extended clutching the Maesteg South token to be surrendered to the signalman. The signalman extends his arms in the same style as the fireman and exchanges the Tondu North token with the fireman's as the engine saunters by with her three coaches.

Returning to the box, further ringing of bells and mysterious rattling noises ensue as again the signalman processes the token and secures Line Clear, this time from Maesteg South. The Up Home signal is replaced, North end loop points changed and Down Starter signal pulled off while a couple of alighting passengers collect a pram from the guard.

8740 pops her whistle in response to the guard's green flag and the train heads off towards Tondu and Bridgend to the crisp bark of the accelerating Pannier as she passes under the bridge onto the single line and recedes into the distance with only a faint haze rising from the exhaust in the hot summer air.

The signalman then crosses the line with the Maesteg South token, lack of which has held the Down train for long enough for some of the more inquisitive passengers on board to crane their heads out of the windows seeking reason for the delay. The token handed safely to the driver, the 55 which has been simmering gently all the while springs to life and barks away into the cutting with her train in the sudden burst of energy characteristic of these engines. The sound dies away to emerge briefly in a deeper roar as the train traverses the points onto the single-line section, then to fade out as a distantly receding and gradually slowing exhaust note up the gradient beyond, while the signalman slowly again climbs into his box. Signals clatter back to on, bells repeat 'Train on Line' in both directions and the little world surrounding the station relapses into the drowsy limbo of the summer afternoon.

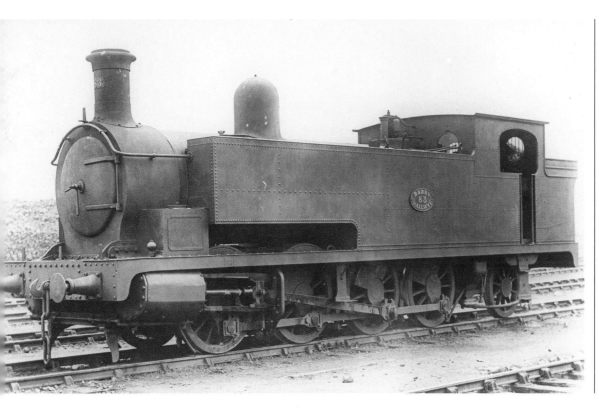

Barry Railway 0-8-2T No. 83 was built by Sharp, Stewart in 1896, was renumbered by the GW 1384 and lasted until July 1930. The Locomotive Superintendent 1888-1905 was J.H. Hosgood. *(Great Western Trust)*

By coincidence, Port Talbot Railway 0-8-2T No. 17 was also built by Sharp, Stewart in 1902, renumbered by the GWR 1358 and lasted until February 1948. The Locomotive Superintendent of the PTR 1896-1905 was W.J. Hosgood, brother of the BR's J.H. Hosgood. *(Great Western Trust)*

Hawksworth's 1500 Class are probably best associated as carriage pilots at Old Oak Common. However, five of the total ten, including 1506 & 1507 recorded here in 1959, were based at Newport Pill. Drivers related that at any speed, they waddled like ducks. Although not the same class of Pannier, perhaps aware of this feature, the Reverend W.T. Awdry named Thomas the Tank Engine's pannier friend 'Duck.' (*Great Western Trust*)

Pill in April 1959 with 1507 'alongside the older 6728' offering a comparison between these two classes of Pannier tanks. (*R.W.A. Jones/ Online Transport Archive*)

Neyland's 1027 *County of Stafford* runs alongside the road between St. Georges and St. Fagans with a Neyland-Paddington parcels on Tuesday 1 June 1954. These services called at every station to pick up or put off consignments which in terms of parcels could range from live pigeons to carpets, mails and small goods. On arrival, it was all hands to the pump to deal with the traffic within the allotted station stop allowance. They were formed of a wide variety of rolling stock and it was not unusual for representatives of the Big Four to be found in the same train. Parcel trains ran throughout the 24-hour period and were often used to convey empty stock if loads permitted as the composition of this train attests. *(D.K. Jones/Cresselley Collection)*

One traffic that was common was of Irish cattle en route to London's Smithfield market. Great care had to be taken to ensure the well-being of the animals. Here at Clarbeston Road, 4962 *Ragley Hall* heads the 2.35pm Cattle Train from Fishguard to Paddington. 13 July 1962. *(D.K. Jones/Cresselley Collection)*

Neyland's 1029 *County of Worcester* passes through the woods to the east of St. Fagans with the 2.35pm Fishguard-Paddington parcels train. Note the mix of six meat vans and containers behind the 'Enparts' Van (M&EE Components). Saturday 14 May 1955. *(D.K. Jones/ Cresselley Collection)*

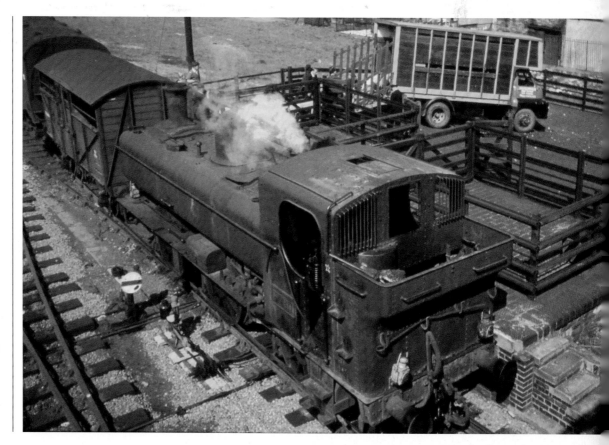

Canton Cattle Dock was one such place en route where animals in transit could be fed and watered. 5784 is seen here, however, berthing a cattle wagon for the conveyance of sheep which are being transferred in April 1961. *(Alan A. Jarvis 0972/Stephenson Locomotive Society)*

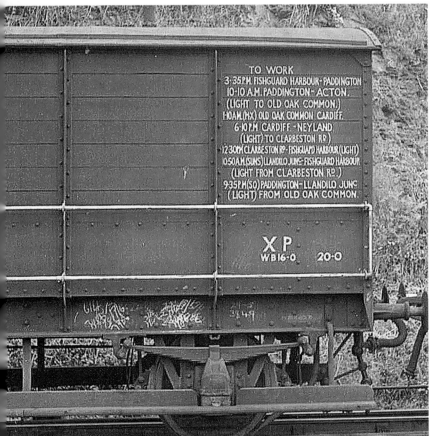

TO WORK
3·35 P.M. FISHGUARD HARBOUR - PADDINGTON
10·10 A.M. PADDINGTON - ACTON
(LIGHT TO OLD OAK COMMON.)
11·0 A.M.(MX) OLD OAK COMMON - CARDIFF.
6·10 P.M. CARDIFF - NEYLAND
(LIGHT) TO CLARBESTON R?.)
12·30 P.M CLARBESTON R? - FISHGUARD HARBOUR (LIGHT)
10·50 A.M.(SUNS) LLANDILO JUNC - FISHGUARD HARBOUR
(LIGHT FROM CLARBESTON R?.)
9·35 P.M.(SO) PADDINGTON - LLANDILO JUNC
(LIGHT) FROM OLD OAK COMMON.

X P
W.B 16·0   20·0

Canton again in 1954 showing a more exotic animal in transit. Nowadays, it is difficult to appreciate that circus movements were often made by rail. Most were made in the hours of darkness to maximise showtime so including this rare shot was irresistible. For the conveyance of elephants, the GW purposely built a strengthened carriage truck specifically for elephants (unfortunately not the one here). Each rolling stock type was given a telegraphic code name to facilitate communication. 'Bloater' provided an obvious link but 'Beetle' for prize cattle vans and in this case 'Python A' for the elephant van is rather interesting.

Seen one Toad, seen them all. The GW had a propensity for stencilling items of rolling stock but W17440 'captured at Milford Haven on 10 July 1962' is surely a classic to prove you wrong. (Alan Wild)

There again, four special brakevans were built and allocated to Branches Fork. 17590 & 17595 are seen here in July 1939. Referred to as 'Noah's Arks' they enabled the traincrew to maintain a clear view ahead when propelling empties up the steep gradients to the nearby collieries on the Cwmffrwdoer and Cwmnantddu branches.

To work the Fish trains from Milford Haven, three main line engines coupled, ran light from Neyland mid-afternoon as the small loco shed at Milford had just two Pannier Tanks. In the 1950/60s, specifically for this traffic and the only allocation in Wales, Neyland had two County Class 4-6-0s along with a handful of Halls. To discourage favouritism (or perhaps encourage bi-lingualism) the GW had a policy of not allocating engines with Welsh names to Welsh Sheds. However, 1020 *County of Monmouth* stands proudly outside her home shed at Neyland on 27 May 1961. At this time maybe Monmouthshire was considered part of England.

Above: A general view of Neyland in 1962. Befitting its status as a terminus a host of stock is on hand, foremost a long raft of fish vans with 'alongside' rakes of parcel vans and passenger brakes then to the right Neyland's modest engine shed.

Below left: The GW recognised the value of publicity and was clearly proud of its involvement at Milford Haven.

Below right: The Trawl Shed at Milford Haven. Here the fish were landed, purchased, crated and loaded into fish vans for conveyance up-country. *(Author's collection)*

The one that got away. Ten ton fish van (telegraphic code name Bloater) 2671, built in 1925 with 18ft wheelbase to Diagram S10. For years, this vehicle had been relegated to departmental use and had languished in the Mileage Siding of Port Talbot Goods Yard as DW150160. Then one day in 1976 it was spotted being towed away for condemnation. Several phone calls later and a scrap value payment of £250 resulted in it passing into the hands of the Great Western Society and is now preserved at Didcot.

Fish traffic, on the same basis as milk, was conveyed in vacuum fitted wagons in order to run at express speeds as a complete train or, as a portion of a passenger train. Originally these were open wagons with some traffic carried in containers. In 1908, specialised vans were introduced similar to the contemporary vans but had slatted (sides and ends) for additional ventilation. The final development being insulated vans.

Milford Haven was one of the largest fishing ports in the country. Here the catch was landed into covered sheds (known as 'Trawl' Sheds) where the buying and selling took place. The fish was loaded into crates and then into the waiting fish vans packed with ice. Traffic was charged by weight. In the 1950s, there were three fish trains per day (M-F) from Milford Haven;

3.20pm to Manchester via Carmarthen conveyed fish traffic for London Midland Region destinations and was worked on to Llandeilo where it connected with the 5.5pm Pontardulais to Crewe (SX) and 4.25pm ex-Swansea Victoria on SO. A BG Neyland to Manchester was conveyed throughout, returning on the 9.50pm ex-York next day. Parcels traffic from Swansea Victoria to Crewe, Stores Van No. 16 from Llanelli to Crewe (TO), attached also at Llandeilo and a Stove R from Swansea to Crewe were also conveyed by this Central Wales service.

3.50pm to Paddington (to Severn Tunnel only in the late 1950s) Engine, Swansea, Treherbert, Aberdare, Merthyr, Porth, Bridgwater, Taunton, Exeter, Plymouth, Penzance, Brakevan (65, 107, 145 or 1144), Sheffield, Salisbury, Weymouth, Bath.

Or, if 5.20pm cancelled Engine, Swansea, Swindon, Paddington, Gloucester, Cardiff, Rhymney, Pontypridd, Merthyr, Newport, Bristol, Bridgwater, Exeter, Kingswear, Plymouth, Penzance, Brakevan (65, 107, 145 or 1144), Sheffield, Salisbury, Weymouth, Bath.

5.20pm Q service to Paddington Engine, Swindon, Birmingham (Moor St), Nantybwch, Brynmawr, Ebbw Vale, Newport, Gloucester, Bristol, Cardiff, Rhymney, Merthyr, Paddington, (Brakevan 98 or 185). At Cardiff Platform 2, a 6-coach passenger set was attached off the previous day's 9.25pm ex-Paddington.

Empty fish vans were worked to Neyland for cleaning before being supplied to Milford Haven for loading and were conveyed on:

4.30pm (SX) Grimsby to Whitland which brought loaded fish vans to Cardiff and Swansea which were then sent forward empty

1.15am (MO) Swindon to Whitland

10.35am Kensington to Neyland

4.55pm Weymouth to Neyland (SX)

4am Marston to Whitland (Suns)

Parcels trains starting at Cardiff for Neyland.

From 1964, British Railways stopped carrying this traffic.

Some of the catch was transported in containers to facilitate intermodal transfer long before the concept of Freightliners. *(Author's collection)*

6912 *Helmster Hall* makes a spirited exit from Milford Haven with the 3.45pm Fish to Severn Tunnel Junction on 10 July 1962. Behind the engine would be loads for Swansea, Treherbert, Aberdare, Merthyr, Porth, Bridgwater, Taunton, Exeter, Plymouth, Penzance, 2 x Brakevans (Nos 65, 107, 145 or 1144), Sheffield, Salisbury, Weymouth & Bath.

As mentioned Neyland supplied all the 'Big Engines' for traffic from Milford Haven as the latter's small shed as seen here housed just two Panniers. 15 July 1962. *(D.K. Jones/ Cresselley Collection)*

4358 brings the 12.45pm Old Oak Common to Neyland to a stand on the Down Relief at Canton. The fireman has removed one of the headlamps changing the classification to light engine. Alongside is 5007 *Rougemont Castle* 'one of Canton's favourites' that will work the train on to Neyland. Meanwhile, on the Up relief 5009 *Shrewsbury Castle* (Swindon Shed) is about to move off with the 3.50pm Whitland to Kensington Milk which had just been re-manned by a Canton crew. 5009 had worked the 1am Paddington to Cardiff and 7.30am Cardiff to Swansea, running light Engine to Felin Fran to relieve the Carmarthen Engine that had worked the Milk from Whitland. 10 December 1955. *(John Hodge)*

5007 *Rougemont Castle* patiently awaits the Guard's 'Right Away' at 7.06pm. She will spend the night on Neyland Shed, run light engine to Milford Haven mid-afternoon then work the 3.50 Milford to Paddington Fish as far as Canton. The 10.35 Kensington Whitland Milk empties and 12.45 Old Oak Neyland Fish empties arrived at Canton one after the other. Loads permitting, the two trains were combined saving engine power and line capacity as is the case here. The consist has three Bloaters with their prominent stepboards, a 6-wheeled Insulated Fish (the last GW designed Fish Van), Passenger Brakevan, 3 Insulated Meat Vans (Micas), a string of Milk Tanks and another Passenger Brakevan bringing up the rear. 10 December 1955. (*John Hodge*)

Another regular traffic from South Wales was Geest Bananas from Barry Dock. Shrewsbury's Jubilee 45651 *Shovell* is recorded here at Palmerston (just to the East of Cadoxton) in 1963 with a string of banana vans forming the 7.10pm Cadoxton Low Level to Crewe. These look like any other type of 10 ton ventilated van but were in fact steam heated. What is not widely appreciated, is that the bananas were green when loaded and the steam heating was a catalyst in the ripening process so that on arrival, they would be an inviting yellow. (*John Hodge*)

Ebbw Junction's 92006 passes through Bridgend on Saturday, 7 July 1962, with a short 9.05am Rogerstone to Landore Class C fitted freight. In 1954, the first eight members of this class were delivered new to Ebbw Junction primarily for working Iron Ore trains to Ebbw Vale. 92006 was withdrawn from Wakefield Shed in April 1967. *(D.K. Jones/Cresselley Collection)*

David Davies was a key figure in the industrialisation of South Wales and Barry in particular. He was born in Llandinam 18 December 1818, the eldest of nine children. Primarily self-educated, he began work as a sawyer and went into agriculture, working alongside his father who died when David was twenty. His first enterprise was the building of a bridge over the Severn at Llandinam and soon built a reputation as a contractor.

From 1855 he was involved in the construction of; 1855 Llanidloes and Newtown Railway, 1858 Vale of Clwyd Railway, 1861 Oswestry and Newtown Railway, 1862 Newtown and Machynlleth Railway, 1863 Pembroke and Tenby Railway (extended to Whitland in 1866), Manchester and 1867 Milford Railway (Pencader to Aberystwyth). In 1866 he became a director of the Brecon and Merthyr Railway.

As a result of his success in the railway trade, Davies became a colliery owner. He was an important figure in the industrialisation of the Rhondda Valley, having founded the Parc and Maendy collieries in the 1860s. He was a Liberal politician who sat in the Commons between 1874 and 1886. In the 1880s, Davies established a limited liability company, the Ocean Coal Company Ltd.

The inability of the Taff Vale Railway and the Bute Docks at Cardiff to cope with the Ocean traffic and the fact that Davies had to pay such high costs to use these facilities, led him to construct new docks at Barry with a railway connection from the Rhondda. The project came to fruition after a lengthy parliamentary process and was completed in 1889. Barry Docks was a crucial factor in the expansion of the South Wales coal trade on a global scale. At the time of Davies's death, 20 July 1890, Ocean Coal was the largest and most profitable coal company in South Wales.

Bridgend: 6810 *Blakemere Grange* departs at 10.53am with the 9.10 SO Llanelly to Bournemouth & Brockenhurst. A Hymek passes on the Down with a Milk Train on Saturday, 15 August 1964. The view is taken from Brackla Street Bridge. As a small child, I was often taken in my pushchair to this vantage point, little realising the crews I waved to were the same I had seen two hours earlier; in the meantime, they had worked to Abergwynfi or Nantymoel. Realising even less that the seed had been sewn leading to a lifetime career as a professional railwayman. *(courtesy Brian Lewis)*

Bridgend a few weeks later on Saturday, 5 September 1964. 6838 *Goodmoor Grange* at 11.07am (16 minutes late) with the same train as in the previous illustration. This marks the end of an era, as it was the very last regular steam worked passenger train from South Wales. *(courtesy Brian Lewis)*

At Ogmore Vale on Tuesday, 26 February 1963, 6676 on Target U8 ran away with a train loaded with coal from Wyndham Colliery Sidings before the brakevan could be attached. The locomotive derailed at Ogmore Vale and came to rest on its side with wheels facing east. The only casualty was a cat. 6676 was recovered by steam crane then removed on 10 March, placed in Tondu Shed on the 11th by being pushed over the Turntable from Ogmore No. 1 Road and ultimately condemned in April 1963. *(Brian Lewis)*

When mishaps occur, contingency measures are arranged. This occasionally results in something out of the ordinary and sometimes there just happens to be an intrepid photographer on hand. Although the circumstances for the diversion are not known, Brian Lewis recorded the following images for posterity when some main line Freights were diverted via Tondu on 6 April 1964. At 3.45pm 6837 *Forthampton Grange* 'just coming off the Llanharan branch' awaits the road through Middle Junction alongside Tondu shed.

6837 gets right-away and looks set to attack the run up to Cefn Junction but in fact stops for water at the end of the Porthcawl platform. Banking engine 4652 can be seen behind the chimney blast.

At 4pm 6837 takes water before continuing with 4652 on the rear to assist.

Then in deteriorating weather at 4.28pm, 6946 *Heatherden Hall* again draws forward to quench her thirst with a train of oil tanks bound for Milford Haven. Once again banker 4652 can be seen behind the guard's van.

The steepest section of the main line is Stormy Bank. The gradient commences just beyond the A48 Overbridge at Pyle seen here and rises west to east for approximately 2 miles, the final 1¼ miles at 1:93. Also beyond the Overbridge was Pyle Sand Siding marking the boundary between the Neath and Newport Districts. Despite being at the beginning of the ascent, Duffryn Yard's 6616 is clearly going to make very heavy weather of the task as she heads for Bridgend but at least makes for a very atmospheric scene on 4 July 1955. *(D.K. Jones/Cresselley Collection)*

5225 heads a train of 36 wagons along the final stretches of Stormy Bank on 14 March 1962 and is banked in rear by an 8750 class Pannier. Stormy Box was under the bridge ahead of the train engine. In deference to the name, a storm is clearly brewing in the east over the worthy citizens of Bridgend. (*R.O. Tuck*)

In stark contrast to the two previous shots and admittedly with a relatively light load of seven coaches, 7021 *Haverfordwest Castle* breasts the top of the bank and passes Stormy Sidings in July 1961 in pure sunshine with a panache so typical of these Swindon Greyhounds. (*Alan A. Jarvis 1011/Stephenson Locomotive Society*)

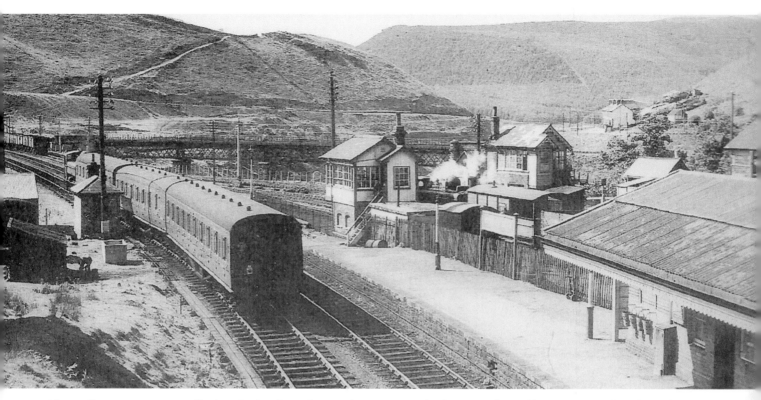

Above: Size was not necessarily the criterion for such an embarrassment of riches as evidenced by Cymmer in the Afan Valley. Served by the R&SB, GW + SWMR it boasted three stations, two signal boxes, a mile long tunnel and two viaducts, one South, one North. A 1957 view of the R&SB station on 5 September as 4675 stands at the head of the empty stock off the 12.45pm from Bridgend. 5787 is shunting between the GW and R&SB signal boxes, both being replaced by a new box on 17 June 1960. The Glyncorrwg Viaduct can be seen in advance of the train with mineral wagons on the upside. *(Great Western Trust)*

Below left: Aberavon Town (R&SBR): a 41XX heads a Treherbert to Swansea service in 1960. Immediately behind the last coach is Aberavon Branch Junction leading to Duffryn Yard and the PTR's main line to Maesteg and the Garw Valley. Ahead of the loco is Plough Junction giving access to Port Talbot General and the SWML. *(D.K. Jones/Cresselley Collection)*

Below right: Same time, same service but in 1959 with 82032. In 1953, ten of these Standards were drafted into the Cardiff Valleys as part of the introduction of Regular Interval Services. They were allocated to Barry, Cathays and Treherbert Sheds lasting until 1957 with the introduction of DMUs so 82032's stay in South Wales is almost at an end. *(D.K. Jones/Cresselley Collection)*

Neath General in 1960. In the Up Bay is the District's Inspection Saloon. Some of the R&SBR services to Treherbert started at Neath from this Bay in order to reduce occupation of the Main Line to Swansea. The same principle applied to most of the services from Pontypool Road over the Vale of Neath. These terminated in the Up Platform and the centre road enabled the locomotive to run round prior to its return service or in some cases continuing on to Swansea. *(D.K. Jones/ Cresselley Collection)*

Neath had a second station here at Riverside which passes beneath the GW Main Line. Although constructed and owned by the VoNR and GW, the station was used by the N&B for its services to/ from Colbren and Brecon. Latterly these ran twice daily with, in addition, a school train to/from Colbren Junction. The two-coach 11.25am to Brecon is seen departing behind 3741 on 4 November 1958. *(D.K. Jones/ Cresselley Collection)*

The approach to Brecon on the N&B was as spectacular as that on the B&M as witness here with 3693 on the 6.20pm from Brecon to Neath alongside Cray Reservoir. Tuesday 4 September 1962. *(Mike Roach)*

At Devynock & Sennybridge 46401 returns light engine off the Brecon to Colbren Goods. *(M.B. Warburton/ Stephenson Locomotive Society)*

Swansea Wind (as in coil) Street Signal Box 5 August 1961 looking north. Passenger services off the Vale of Neath terminated here from 1863 to 1873. The left fork is the North Dock Branch and reached the SWML adjacent to Swansea High Street station. The right-hand fork is the VoN leading to Danygraig and beyond. Behind the photographer is an end-on Junction to South Dock and the LNWR. *(Great Western Trust)*

A 1929 aerial view of Swansea High Street with the North Dock Branch alongside.

Opposite above: Nestled between High Street station and the North Dock Branch was located an Engine Lay-By seen here with 5091 *Cleeve Abbey* (rebuilt from its namesake Star Class in 1938) & behind, an unidentified Hall on 15 September 1962.

Opposite below: Swansea High Street looking west with its lovely semaphores in 1972. Extension of Multiple Aspect signalling in 1976 transferred control of the area to Port Talbot and rendered High Street Signal Box (right of centre) and semaphores redundant.

Below: Reversal at Swansea facilitated the detachment of the dining car section (3/4 coaches) marshalled next to the incoming engine on arrival of Down trains, whilst a fresh locomotive was attached at the other end to the remaining eight West Wales coaches (four for each destination). Here, in this view, snaking around the dining car portion waiting to be attached, 7306 draws the West Wales portion of the Up Pembroke Coast Express into platform 4 in September 1957.

With the reconstruction of Swansea High Street all West Wales services called there from 1926 thereby reducing the status of Landore High Level. The only exceptions to this were the Fishguard Harbour Boat trains when operated exclusive of any other West Wales portion (Summer timetable). These were Up services at 3.55am (Sleeper) & 4.55am from Fishguard and 11.35am ex Paddington travelling via the Swansea District Line calling at Llanelli and Cardiff.

Post-war, the multi-portioned West Wales service formations were more complex than their West Country Counterparts. Individual services did not include sections for all three destinations (i.e., Fishguard, Neyland, and Pembroke Dock). Cardigan and Milford Haven were usually served by a connection at Whitland and Johnston, respectively. The regular combination was Neyland plus a portion for Fishguard or Pembroke Dock and sometimes a Carmarthen contingent. The basic timetable pattern remained until September 1963 when through coaches beyond Swansea ended.

When the Oystermouth Railway, later known as the Swansea & Mumbles (S&MR), commenced a passenger service on 25 March 1807, South Wales saw the first fare paying passengers in the world. The Mumbles Railway ultimately employed the largest trams in the UK. Thirteen in number, they were built by the Brush Company at Loughborough and had seating for 106 passengers. They could run coupled allowing their legitimate description of trains. Swansea Car Shed at Rutland Street is seen here on 16 October 1959. *(R.O. Tuck)*

Mumbles Railway Terminus at Swansea Rutland Street with No. 9 on 16 October 1959. *(R.O. Tuck)*

This rare nugget is the R&SBR terminus at Swansea Riverside circa 1920. The R&SBR, PTR and SWMR were worked by the GW from 1908 and 1076 Class 852 of East Dock Shed waits to depart with a train for Treherbert composed of TV, R&SBR and GW coaching stock. A major reorganisation of the system in the Swansea Docks area in 1926 resulted in Riverside and East Dock stations closing in 1930 and the passenger services all concentrated on High Street. *(Great Western Trust)*

Before 1923, Swansea Harbour Trust together with Powlesland & Mason were responsible for all shunting within Swansea docks. Due to the network's tight curvatures, large numbers of 0-4-0 tanks were employed and this trio, outside Swansea East Dock shed in 1958, is representative. They also reflect their parentage, 1140 (SHT Andrew Barclay 1905), 1144 (SHT Hawthorn Leslie 1909) and 1152 (P&M Peckett 1912). *(R.W.A. Jones/Online Transport Archive)*

Swansea Victoria (the LNWR Terminus) is seen here as 80099 waits to depart with the 9.45am to Shrewsbury on 25 April 1963 and, alongside, 3604 on station pilot duties. The station was down on the waterfront where today the Marina can be found. The overall roof was partially destroyed by the Luftwaffe, the remaining glass removed as a safety precaution, never to be replaced. Closure took place on 13 June 1964. To the right of the picture were the High-Level lines leading to Wind Street and the GW. *(Alan A. Jarvis 2205/ Stephenson Locomotive Society)*

Swansea was served by six Railways; GW, LNW, MR, R&SBR, S&MR and apart from London had more termini than anywhere else in the country. High Street (GW), Victoria (LNW), St Thomas (MR), Riverside (R&SBR), East Dock (GW) and Russell Street (Mumbles Railway). Swansea St Thomas was the Midland Railway's modest terminus, a far-removed enclave of the parent company with its nearest point of contact at Three Cocks Junction. Initially, through trains were operated from Hereford (only possible with running rights over Cambrian, Brecon & Merthyr and Neath & Brecon Railway metals) but these were discontinued in 1931. 2 July 1955. *(Alan A. Jarvis 0612/Stephenson Locomotive Society)*

Between Swansea Victoria and Pontardulais, at the extreme western end of the Gower peninsula, the LNW had a branch from Gowerton to Llanmorlais. Penclawdd is noted for its cockles and there is a local expression, 'A mouth like a Penclawdd cockle woman'. Here at Penclawdd, a Pannier is recorded with the 11.20am Goods from Gowerton South on 2 August 1957.

At Pontardulais Junction 4676 arrives in June 1963 with a local service from Swansea Victoria. As the Running-In board suggests, connections were made to/from Llanelly. With the closure of the LNW to Swansea Victoria in 1964, Central Wales Line services to Shrewsbury continued but to/from Swansea High Street which now, ironically, involves a reversal at Llanelly. *(Alan A. Jarvis 2663/ Stephenson Locomotive Society)*

Llanelly Old Castle Crossing just west of Llanelly, where an industrial line between North Dock and the Oldcastle Tinplate Works made a flat crossing with the SWML. The Llanelly & Mynydd Mawr Railway had its terminus and Offices on the right of the picture taken on 26 July 1960. (*Great Western Trust*)

GW Official Photo of Llanelly Docks dated 1921. Llanelly was on the edge of the Coalfield and limit of heavy industry presenting a defining line between South and West Wales. (*Author's collection*)

The 30 members of the Class 380 0-8-4T, although designed under the LNWR by H.P.M. Beames, appeared as LMS locomotives soon after the 1923 grouping. They were essentially an extended version of the 1185 Class 0-8-2T with a longer bunker and their main area of work was in South Wales. Numbered 7930–7959, withdrawal began in 1944. Only two survived long enough to be renumbered 47931 and 47937 under BR, the last being withdrawn in 1951. *(Great Western Trust)*

The former LNW Swansea Paxton Street shed is host to G2A 49035 in 1953. Built 13 April 1898, she was withdrawn from Paxton Street 31 January 1957. *(LCGB)*

The Shed at Llandovery reflects its joint status, the 8Fs an asset for working heavy Freights to the Midlands and Northwest. 16 May 1964. *(Alan A. Jarvis 2785/Stephenson Locomotive Society)*

Llandovery seen here sometime in 1960. *(D.K. Jones/Cresselley Collection)*

Llandilo on the LNW's Central Wales line in 1958 with a 74XX and a service for Carmarthen. North to Llandovery was GW/LNW Joint, West to Carmarthen (Abergwili Junction) LNW and South to Pontardulais GW where LNW metals were regained onwards to Swansea Victoria or Llanelli (Llandeilo Junction).

Another variation on a theme. Toad 56722 'built to diagram AA15 in 1919' is viewed here in 1960. The need for its specific attachment to the Newcastle Emlyn branch is intriguing. (*R.W.A. Jones/Online Transport Archive*)

North of Carmarthen, the GW's line to Aberystwyth diverged from the LNW's branch to Llandilo at Abergwili Junction. The largest intermediate point was Lampeter where, on 26 April 1963, we see 2224 with a train for Carmarthen crossing a freight but not a milk tank in sight even though marshalling of milk tanks for Felin Fach and Pont Llanio Dairies was a major feature here. *(Alan A. Jarvis 1337/Stephenson Locomotive Society)*

At Pont Llanio we see 2224 again on 26 April 1963. To the left of the picture is the large dairy with direct rail connection. Shunting was often performed by the train engine of the passenger services. The layout was very restricted and gives little idea of what this entailed. *(Alan A. Jarvis 2191/Stephenson Locomotive Society)*

Crossing the River Towy at the north end of Carmarthen with an impressive bracket signal, 7401 departs with a service for Llandilo on 11 September 1952.

A busy scene at the North end of Carmarthen on 18 August 1961. On the extreme left can be seen milk tanks in the Dairy Loading Bay, then 2298 with an arrival from the west, 6843 *Poulton Grange* detaching from a Down freight, 5027 *Farleigh Castle* with a Down Paddington service and in the bay, another 2251 Class.

Carmarthen Junction station opened in 1852 and closed in 1926. It was some way from the town centre with poor road access. The Carmarthen and Cardigan Railway opened the present station in 1860. This is situated on the apex of a triangle necessitating reversal of main line services which diverged at Myrtle Hill Junction. In the early years of the twentieth century, Slip coaches were employed on some trains to avoid the time-consuming process entailed with the reversal. 7811 *Dunley Manor* waits to depart for Pembroke Dock on 26 April 1963. *(Alan A. Jarvis 2200/Stephenson Locomotive Society)*

Heading west, we regain the main line at Carmarthen Bridge Junction seen here immediately before the bridge on 5 September 1962. The Bascule bridge over the River Towy was built in 1911 by the Cleveland Bridge and Engineering Company; it last opened in 1950. Beyond this was another milk factory at Johnstown. *(Alan A. Jarvis 1795/Stephenson Locomotive Society)*

Headboard of the Pembroke Coast Express with the heraldic crests of Tenby (left) and Pembroke (right). The PCE was the senior South Wales Express in more ways than one. The 1928 timetable first identified the 9.20am from Pembroke Dock as the 'Tenby and Carmarthen Bay Express'. The corresponding Down train left Paddington at 9.55am within the already established XX55 departure pattern for South Wales services. It had the fastest of all schedules, beating the 'Red Dragon', 'Capitals United' and even the 'South Wales Pullman' (the latter by five minutes).

An aerial view of Whitland looking East. The United Dairies factory is centre, the loco shed to the right of the station with its bays for Pembroke (right) and Cardigan (left). After reversal at Swansea, the second at Carmarthen was expedited by 'Topping and Tailing.' This Carmarthen or Neyland locomotive would then work through to destination, with an additional locomotive used from Whitland for the Pembroke portion or at Clarbeston Road for Fishguard. This resulted in Whitland and Fishguard based engines rarely venturing off either branch.

Departing Whitland with four coaches forming the Neyland portion of the Down PCE (8.55am from Paddington) is 7320 on 22 August 1962. The Pembroke section will have been detached in the platform awaiting its engine.

At Whitland, Centenary Brake Third W6653 is recorded on 9 July 1962. These vehicles were built in 1935 for the centenary of the GWR to the full 9ft 7in width of the GW's loading gauge, specifically for the prestigious Cornish Riviera Express. They were not permitted to run off the GW and even then, a red triangular plate mounted on the solebar stated the restriction 'Not to run over the Eastern & Western Valleys, North of Saltney Junction or between Little Mill Junction and Maindee Junction'. There are several contemporary photographs of this vehicle in West Wales but no mention of how it got there. On to a good thing, the locals clearly adopted the maxim of 'finder's keepers'. *(Author's collection)*

A regular traffic on the Pembroke & Tenby line was military vehicles to and from the Castle Martin firing range used for training purposes. Only light vehicles are visible in this illustration but there may be tanks or heavier armoured vehicles within the consist justifying the power of 4250 here on 7 July 1962.

An early twentieth century view of Narberth showing the substantial station building and Goods Shed behind. *(Author's collection)*

NARBERTH STATION PEM.

The wrought iron canopy supports at Tenby are possibly unique and provide an easy means of identification in photographs. *(Author's collection)*

A 1958 view of Tenby looking north as 8107 approaches. Non-corridor stock in West Wales is unusual as the Swansea District had no allocation of these. A train of empty stock can be seen stabled on the Viaduct Siding, one of only two options at Tenby. *(James S. Doubleday)*

Pembroke Dock on 24 August 1963 with 7804 *Baydon Manor* arriving with the Down PCE. Behind the photographer the line continues into the Admiralty Dockyard complex.

Despite its modest track layout, the still extant station building is an attractive design. 20 August 1987. *(Author's Collection)*

Above left: Pembroke Dock Shed and Carriage sidings in 1958. To the left of the Shed, there was a connection to the Army Ordnance Depot at Hobbs Point. (*D.K. Jones/Cresselley Collection*)

Above right: On 7 January 1908, the GW introduced the first Road Motor Service in Wales from Llandyssul to New Quay. Eventually, a number of services were operated throughout South Wales filling gaps that were by now too costly to develop by extending the rail network. The GW Road Motor Services were merged with South Wales Commercial Motors to become the Western Welsh Omnibus Company ('Western' reflecting the parentage) in 1929.

Below: With a service from Whitland, 1622 arrives at Cardigan with its one coach passenger train on 16 June 1962. (*Alan A. Jarvis 1520/ Stephenson Locomotive Society*)

Alongside the banks of the River Teifi and under clear blue skies, 5520 comes off Cardigan shed after servicing to work the 5.45pm to Whitland on 16 June 1962. *(Alan A. Jarvis 1323/Stephenson Locomotive Society)*

1648 is captured in the rustic surroundings so typical of the Cardigan branch, departing from Kilgerran with a service from Whitland on 20 August 1962. *(R.W.A. Jones/Online Transport Archive)*

At Llanglydwen 4558 & 1648 cross with trains from and to Cardigan respectively on 16 June 1962. 4557 & 4558 were shedded at Whitland for many years and several photographs show them double-heading on the Cardigan Branch, not through train load but to achieve an engine working balance. *(Alan A. Jarvis 1538/Stephenson Locomotive Society)*

In 1907, four sleeping cars, 9082-9085, were built to the 70ft Dreadnought design for overnight services to West Wales. They were fitted with 6-wheel bogies to improve riding qualities for the potential 24 occupants but weighed in at 40 tons as a result. *(Great Western Trust)*

Above: In connection with the sailings from Fishguard, through trains were run from Paddington with limited stops and full dining services. For the rest of the day, the more usual link was a change of trains at Clarbeston Road as here, with 9602 taking water in June 1958 having just arrived from Fishguard. *(M.B. Warburton/Stephenson Locomotive Society)*

Below left: In 1909 the GW promoted its new services to Ireland with Day Excursions to Killarney. *(Great Western Trust)*

Below right: At Cardiff 3408 *Killarney* (renamed for the purpose) poses with a Fishguard boat train in 1907. The five coaches are 70ft stock. Four, because of their recessed door design, were referred to as the concertina stock and the dining car a dreadnought, so called because the introduction of this type of vehicle coincided with the launch of HMS *Dreadnought,* a new battleship of the grand fleet.

The dining car in the previous photograph was one of twelve numbered 9534-9545 to lot 1131 of 1907. 9544 is the actual one included here. *(Great Western Trust)*

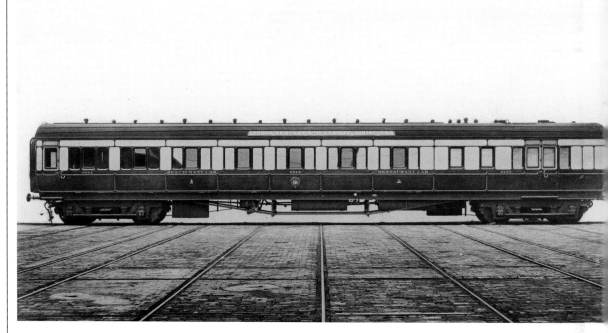

The redevelopment of Fishguard in 1906 made provision for extensive siding facilities, seen here alongside the main running lines and Pannier 5716 in June 1957. *(Great Western Trust)*

Fishguard Harbour viewed 4 March 1926. In 1906 the GW blasted 2m tons of rock in order to expand its facilities at Fishguard including a new station, Goods depot and, visible in the foreground, lairage for cattle. *(Great Western Trust)*

The GW's Fishguard Bay Hotel was described in its brochure as a 'Piscatorial Paradise.' Only the GW could have come up with that one! Cunard's transatlantic liners calling at Fishguard were to be scheduled on a regular basis affording the fastest transit from New York to London. RMS *Mauretania* made the first landing on 30 August 1909. The connecting express, double headed by outside framed 4-4-0s 3402 *Halifax* and 4108 *Gardenia*, reached Cardiff in 2 hours 7 minutes, an all-time record.

Our journey through this Gallery started with a French invasion. Finally, one for the next quiz, in February 1797 at Fishguard, another French invasion was attempted, the last time hostile troops set foot on British soil. *(Author's collection)*